Game Development with MonoGame

Build a 2D Game Using Your Own Reusable and Performant Game Engine

Louis Salin
Rami Morrar

Apress®

Game Development with MonoGame

Louis Salin
Cedar Park, TX, USA

Rami Morrar
San Leandro, CA, USA

ISBN-13 (pbk): 978-1-4842-7770-6
https://doi.org/10.1007/978-1-4842-7771-3

ISBN-13 (electronic): 978-1-4842-7771-3

Managing Director, Apress Media LLC: Welmoed Spahr
Acquisitions Editor: Spandana Chatterjee
Development Editor: Laura Berendson
Coordinating Editor: Divya Modi

Cover designed by eStudioCalamar

Cover image designed by Pixabay

Distributed to the book trade worldwide by Springer Science+Business Media New York, 1 New York Plaza, Suite 4600, New York, NY 10004-1562, USA. Phone 1-800-SPRINGER, fax (201) 348-4505, e-mail orders-ny@springer-sbm.com, or visit www.springeronline.com. Apress Media, LLC is a California LLC and the sole member (owner) is Springer Science + Business Media Finance Inc (SSBM Finance Inc). SSBM Finance Inc is a **Delaware** corporation.

For information on translations, please e-mail booktranslations@springernature.com; for reprint, paperback, or audio rights, please e-mail bookpermissions@springernature.com.

Apress titles may be purchased in bulk for academic, corporate, or promotional use. eBook versions and licenses are also available for most titles. For more information, reference our Print and eBook Bulk Sales web page at www.apress.com/bulk-sales.

Any source code or other supplementary material referenced by the author in this book is available to readers on GitHub via the book's product page, located at www.apress.com/978-1-4842-7770-6. For more detailed information, please visit www.apress.com/source-code.

Printed on acid-free paper

Dedicated to my family and friends who keep pushing me forward.

– Rami Morrar

Table of Contents

About the Authors

Louis Salin has been a developer for more than 15 years in a wide variety of fields, developing on Windows in the early days in C, C++, and eventually C#. He also worked as a developer on Linux-based web applications using different scripting languages such as Ruby and Python. His early love for coding comes from all the time he spent as a kid copying video games written in Basic from books borrowed from the library. He wrote his first game in high school and took many classes in computer graphics.

 **Rami Morrar** is a self-taught game developer with a few years of development experience under his belt. Morrar spent his days as a young kid hacking his Nintendo consoles with homebrew software. In his early adult years, he delved into languages mostly found in the family of C programming, such as C# and C++. He is a freelance technology writer who reviews games and writes tutorials on MonoGame. He is currently working on his own independent project in the framework as well.

About the Technical Reviewer

Andrey Talanin is a fourth-year student getting a bachelor's degree in software engineering at Higher School of Economics, a public research university in the Russian Federation. He is a backend developer currently working with .NET Core, ASP.NET Core, and Transact SQL. He started playing around with C# at the age of 16. Nowadays Andrey is building a web developer career with C# as it is a perfect language for modern enterprise applications. Meanwhile, he is keeping an eye on some pet projects, many of which are games or game libraries created with the MonoGame framework (formerly Microsoft XNA).

Acknowledgments

I have to thank the people on the MonoGame forums and Discord servers for providing their knowledge and help with this book. I wouldn't have been able to do it without their help.

Thanks also to my close friends and family who kept pushing me on to finish. I don't think I would have pulled through without their support.

– Rami Morrar

Introduction

This is a sequel to the original *MonoGame Mastery* book. If you haven't read the original, I highly recommend checking it out before you get into this one. This book has more intermediate techniques, ranging from putting different languages into a game to setting up for debugging. At the end, we will also be talking about notable libraries that will help make development easier in MonoGame.

By the end of the book, you will have a better knowledge of programming in MonoGame and utilizing the Content Pipeline tool for more efficiency. In the first half of the book, you will be looking at the previous 2D shooter and improving it with a level editor. In the second half, you will be making a small 2D platformer that utilizes a texture shader and particle engine. You will also look at notable libraries (along with their GitHub links) to see their source code and what they do. We hope you'll find this book useful for your programming endeavors.

CHAPTER 1

Game Performance

The first step on your journey to turn a game concept into a fun and enjoyable game is to take a look at your game performance and improve it. Game performance should always be in the back of your mind as you develop your game. The reason for this is that a slow running game has a disastrous effect on the player's enjoyment of the game. From skipped frames that hinder the player's ability to aim a weapon and shoot enemies to game stuttering that makes the game unusable, bad game performance is something that should be avoided at all costs.

As your starting point, take the game developed in the *MonoGame Mastery* book, published by Apress. In that book, a game engine and core loop were created. In this book, you'll take them to the next level. The code for that game is located here: `https://github.com/Apress/monogame-mastery`.

In this chapter, you will learn

- How to measure game performance

- How to handle skipped frames

- How to managing memory using game object pools

© Louis Salin and Rami Morrar 2022
L. Salin and R. Morrar, *Game Development with MonoGame*,
https://doi.org/10.1007/978-1-4842-7771-3_1

Measuring Game Performance

In order to seamlessly detect movement in a series of images displayed on a screen, as in the case of animations or video games, the images must be displayed in succession at a pace that is rapid enough to fool the human eye. Any slower than that and the eye will have time to see each image on its own and fail to connect them together as a fluid animation. Think of flipbook animations, where each sheet of paper in the booklet has a single image. If you flip the pages in rapid succession, using your thumbs to control the speed, your brain will meld all the images together into the illusion of movement if the speed is fast enough. Each image in the flipbook is called a frame, and how fast those frames are displayed is measured in frames per second.

Experts generally agree that the human eye will see movement when the frames per second (shortened to FPS) are between 30 and 60. Anything slower than 30 FPS will cause a feeling that the game is lagging or stuttering. Anything faster than 60 FPS, on the other hand, does not improve the smoothness of the animation. In summary, your games should ideally display between 30 and 60 images per second on the screen.

There is more to this story, however. When using MonoGame, whenever a frame is drawn on the screen, the framework calls both the game's Update() and Draw() methods, meaning they have to both execute in a timely fashion to achieve the desired number of frames per second. As you know, the Update() method is used to compute changes in the state of the game and take into account player inputs, like pulling on the trigger to shoot an enemy. How often the Update() method is called determines how responsive the game is to the player. It could also be argued that a player whose Update() method is called more often per second will have an advantage over a player with a slower frame rate. In some competitive games, higher frame rates have shown to increase a player's kill-to-death ratio (KDR), an indicator of how many times a player dies in a match compared to how many kills they have achieved. So more FPS is better, even if the human eye doesn't perceive much difference on the screen.

Unless you bought a high-end gaming monitor, your computer screen likely has a refresh rate of 60 hertz (Hz), which is a measure of how many times per second the monitor is able to refresh the image on screen. If it sounds similar to FPS, that's because it is! With a 60 Hz monitor, every 1/60th of a second an image is displayed on the screen, drawn from top to bottom very quickly. This method of displaying images is important. The graphics card tells the monitor what to draw, but it takes a certain amount of time to draw it, as each pixel, from top to bottom, is lit up on the monitor. If in the middle of the drawing process the graphic card tells the monitor to draw another image, the monitor will not go back to lighting up pixels from the top. Instead, it will start drawing the new image from where it stopped drawing the last image. If the two frames are slightly different, because the player moved in the game, it will cause tearing, as demonstrated in Figure 1-1, where an image being drawn has two tearing points, indicating that the monitor was asked to draw three images during a single refresh, each shown from three different points of view, which can be due to a game character moving laterally.

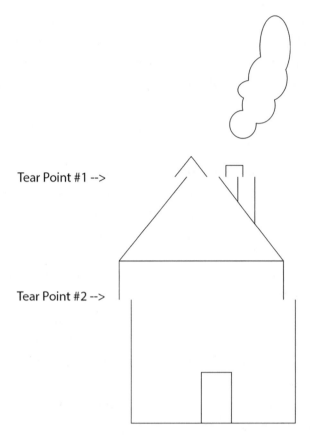

Figure 1-1. *An image with two tearing points*

To avoid any tearing effects, the game's FPS should ideally match the monitor's refresh rate so new images are always drawn starting at the top of the monitor. Matching when images are sent to the monitor is not something you have to care about, because MonoGame and the graphics card will handle the details. However, you need to ensure that your game can run at the desired number of frames per seconds or gracefully degrade the game's computations to enable it to run at an acceptable speed. Note that playing at 30 FPS on a 60 Hz monitor will work because the monitor will be able to draw the same image twice before the game sends it a new image. However, it means that the game will feel less responsive to the player.

Why is all this important? Because MonoGame by default runs at 60 FPS and will try to call the Update() method 60 times per second and try to call the Draw() method at least that many times per second as well. This last statement is important. MonoGame will try to call Update() 60 times per second and may skip the Draw() calls if the frame rate is dropping due to excessive computations or drawing time. It is more important to maintain a correct game state and allow the player input to be computed than to draw to the screen consistently. For example, if a game object moves at a speed of, say, 10 units per frame and its position in the game scene is updating at every call to Update(), you want that position to be updated consistently, 60 times per second. If you did not have this guarantee, you would need to calculate the new position of the game object at every frame based on how much time has passed between the current frame and the previous one or risk having game objects that move at different speeds on different machines whenever the game slows down. When the game slows down, MonoGame assumes it is because the Draw() method is slow and will skip it in an attempt to catch up.

As you'll see below, you have control over the framework's ability to synchronize with the monitor refresh rate and you also can change your game's FPS.

Inspecting the Game Performance

There are a few things you can do to measure the performance of your game. The easiest method is to use the integrated diagnostics tools that come with your development environment, if available. The code for this project was written using Visual Studio, which includes a CPU and memory monitor that gets updated in real time as the game runs in debug mode. Figure 1-2 shows the game's memory profile after just five seconds of execution. This tool is useful to detect memory leaks, an indication of objects being created and remaining in memory for longer than they should, and to detect garbage collection runs by the .Net Framework, which can ruin game performance and cause stuttering while they occur. Garbage collection can be seen in Figure 1-2 by the little inverted bullet shaped icon at the top of the memory graph.

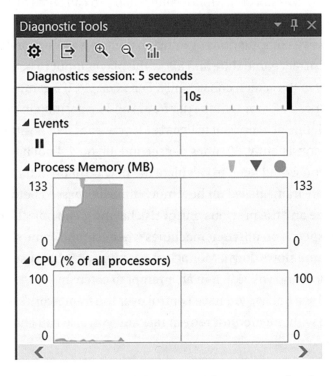

Figure 1-2. *Memory usage of the game after 5 seconds of execution*

Another way to measure the game's performance is to compute statistics over time. As discussed, it would be useful to show at runtime how many frames per seconds are being generated by the game. But because that metric changes so quickly, you could also track a rolling average of FPS measurements over the last sixty frames by keeping track of past measurements. Other useful statistics to track could be the minimum and maximum FPS in your rolling window and the number of times the Draw() and Update() methods are called, because in an ideal world they should be called the same number of times.

To track those measurements, you will update the existing game codebase and add a new game object responsible for tracking frames per seconds and the number of times Update() and Draw() are called. Then you will add that new object to the MainGameState class and put it on the screen when the _debug flag of the BaseGameState class is set to true.

First, let's create the class:

```
public class StatsObject : BaseTextObject
{
    public const int ROLLING_SIZE = 60;
    private Queue<float> _rollingFPS = new Queue<float>();

    public float FPS { get; set; }
    public float MinFPS { get; private set; }
    public float MaxFPS { get; private set; }
    public float AverageFPS { get; private set; }
    public bool IsRunningSlowly { get; set; }
    public int NbUpdateCalled { get; set; }
    public int NbDrawCalled { get; set; }

    public StatsObject(SpriteFont font) : base(font)
    {
        NbUpdateCalled = 0;
        NbDrawCalled = 0;
    }

    public void Update(GameTime gameTime)
    {
        NbUpdateCalled++;
        FPS = 1.0f / (float) gameTime.ElapsedGameTime.
        TotalSeconds;
        _rollingFPS.Enqueue(FPS);
```

```csharp
        if (_rollingFPS.Count > ROLLING_SIZE)
        {
            _rollingFPS.Dequeue();
            var sum = 0.0f;
            MaxFPS = int.MinValue;
            MinFPS = int.MaxValue;
            foreach (var fps in _rollingFPS.ToArray())
            {
                sum += fps;
                if (fps > MaxFPS)
                {
                    MaxFPS = fps;
                }

                if (fps < MinFPS)
                {
                    MinFPS = fps;
                }
            }
            AverageFPS = sum / _rollingFPS.Count;
        }
        else
        {
            AverageFPS = FPS;
            MinFPS = FPS;
            MaxFPS = FPS;
        }
    }
```

```
public override void Render(SpriteBatch spriteBatch)
{
    NbDrawCalled++;
    base.Render(spriteBatch);
}
}
```

The class above is a game object, which means it can be drawn on the screen. Every time the Render() method is called, via the main Draw() method in the main game loop, it will increment the NbDrawCalled counter. Similarly, every time the Update() method is called, it will increment the NbUpdateCalled counter and calculate the statistics you care about. First, it will calculate the current FPS value by dividing 1.0 by gameTime.ElapsedGameTime.TotalSeconds, which is the number of seconds that has passed since the last call to Update(). This is provided by MonoGame and should be a value that is smaller than 1. Since you aim for 60 frames per second, you expect gameTime.ElapsedGameTime.TotalSeconds to be roughly equal to 1.0 divided by 60, so 0.01667. Dividing 1 by 0.10667 gets you 60 FPS. Then, you store the FPS in a queue that will fill up until it contains 60 elements. Once that happens, the code will continuously add a new FPS value in the queue and pop the oldest element out of it so the queue only contains the most recent 60 FPS values. It then calculates the average FPS over the last 60 measurements, the smallest FPS value, and the biggest FPS value. Finally, it reuses the base class' Text property and creates the final string that will be displayed on the screen. It looks like this:

```
FPS: 60.000237
Avg FPS: 60.000168
Running Slowly: false
Nb Updates: 1701
Nb Draws: 1700
```

The variable `IsRunningSlowly` is also given to you by MonoGame and is set to true when the framework detects that your game is not keeping up. Note also that `NbUpdateCalled` and `NbDrawCalled` can be off by 1 when you observe them because it is very likely that you took the measurements after an update, but before a draw call, or vice-versa.

The `StatsObject` class, which can be added to the game's engine so it can be used in future projects, derives from the engine's `BaseTextObject` class, which has the ability to draw text on the screen, but it requires a `SpriteFont`, a special kind of asset that is used to render fonts. The game already has two `SprintFonts` included in it but the size of the fonts are too big for your purposes, so let's create a new `SpriteFont`.

In the Content Pipeline Tool, create a new `SpriteFont` called Stats in the `Fonts` folder, as shown in Figure 1-3.

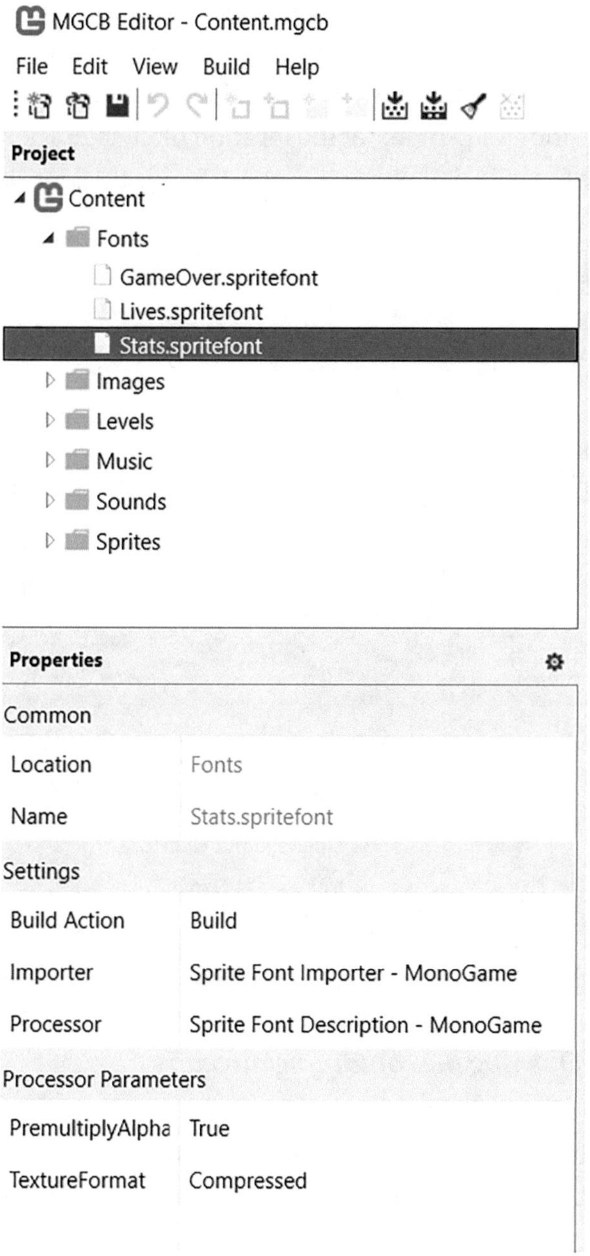

MGCB Editor - Content.mgcb

File   Edit   View   Build   Help

Project

▲ Content
   ▲ Fonts
      GameOver.spritefont
      Lives.spritefont
      Stats.spritefont
   ▷ Images
   ▷ Levels
   ▷ Music
   ▷ Sounds
   ▷ Sprites

Properties

Common

| Location | Fonts |
| Name | Stats.spritefont |

Settings

Build Action	Build
Importer	Sprite Font Importer - MonoGame
Processor	Sprite Font Description - MonoGame

Processor Parameters

| PremultiplyAlpha | True |
| TextureFormat | Compressed |

Figure 1-3. *Adding a new SpriteFont*

Now open the file that was generated by this SpriteFont to edit the size of the font. Right-click on the SpriteFont in the Content Pipeline Tool and select Open Containing Directory, as shown in Figure 1-4. This will open up the Windows Explorer at the location of the file. Then edit the Stats.spritefont file that was generated. Change the font size to 10, like this:

```
<Size>10</Size>
```

Save and close the file, and then build the asset content pipeline.

Figure 1-4. *Opening the containing directory*

You now need to add the new game object to your game. Open the MainGameState.cs file and add the following private variables to the class:

```
private const string StatsFont = "Fonts/Stats";
private StatsObject _statsText;
```

Then instantiate the StatsObject class in the LoadContent() method:

```
_statsText = new StatsObject(LoadFont(StatsFont));
_statsText.Position = new Vector2(10, 10);

if (_debug)
{
    AddGameObject(_statsText);
}
```

This will create the game object and position it near the top left corner of the screen. Then you only add it to the list of game objects being rendered if the base class' _debug flag is set to true.

Finally, in the UpdateGameState() method, add the following code:

```
if (_debug)
{
    _statsText.Update(gameTime);
}
```

This will call the Update() method only when the _debug flag is true. Set the flag to true and run the game. Figure 1-5 shows you what you should see.

Figure 1-5. *Game stats displayed on the screen*

The GameTime Class

As you are aware, MonoGame will call the Update() and Draw() methods and pass in a GameTime parameter. Any class inheriting from the Game class will override those two functions:

```
protected virtual void Draw(GameTime gameTime);
protected virtual void Update(GameTime gameTime);
```

As you have already seen, this GameTime class is extremely useful for debugging purposes due to the following parameters that it provides:

- TotalGameTime

- ElapsedGameTime

- IsRunningSlowly

The TotalGameTime keeps track of the amount of time that the game has been running and is a TimeSpan, which includes two sets of properties you can use to inspect it. First, you have the set of properties that start with the word "Total," like TotalMinutes and TotalSeconds. They take the entire timespan and convert it to the desired units. For example, a timespan of one hour would yield 60 TotalMinutes. Similarly, a timespan of 1 minute would yield 0.01667 TotalHours. The second set of properties is the Days, Hours, Minutes, Seconds, and Milliseconds properties. They give you a specific part of the timespan. For example, a total game time of 1 hour, 47 minutes and 10 seconds would yield zero Days, 1 Hours, 47 Minutes, 10 Seconds, and 0 Milliseconds.

ElapsedGameTime is also a timespan, but it is used to calculate the time taken between two Update() calls or two Draw() calls.

Finally, `IsRunningSlowly` is a parameter that is set by MonoGame to indicate that the framework is skipping frames in an attempt to catch up to maintain the desired FPS settings. As a developer, you could use this flag to protect resource-intensive parts of the game, like maybe turning off some particle effects.

You will use the `GameTime` object below as you learn various strategies to control the FPS of the game.

Controlling the Game's FPS Settings

Out of the box, MonoGame will try to run the game at 60 FPS. But it may not always be able to do so, or the developers of the game may want to control the FPS settings themselves. All in all, you have a few options at your disposal, which can be used in conjunction with each other:

- You let MonoGame run at 60 FPS by default.

- You tell MonoGame to synchronize itself to the monitor's refresh rate

- You tell MonoGame not to synchronize with the monitor's refresh rate.

- You tell MonoGame to use a fixed time step, which is the amount of time each frame will take. If a frame finishes updating and drawing early, MonoGame will pause to fill the remaining available time.

- You tell MonoGame to run as fast as it can.

To tell MonoGame to synchronize with the monitor's refresh rate, you need to set the `GraphicsDeviceManager`'s `SynchronizeWithVerticalRetrace` flag to true or false, as done in `MainGame.cs`.

```
protected override void Initialize()
{
    graphics.PreferredBackBufferWidth = _Designed
    ResolutionWidth;
    graphics.PreferredBackBufferHeight = _Designed
    ResolutionHeight;
    graphics.IsFullScreen = false;
    graphics.SynchronizeWithVerticalRetrace = false;
    graphics.ApplyChanges();
}
```

On the other hand, MonoGame's fixed time step is used to force the
game to spend exactly the same amount of time per frame. So if you
want to force the game to run at 50 FPS for some reason, you could tell
MonoGame to use a fixed time step of 0.02 seconds so that every seconds,
50 frames have gone by. This is accomplished by setting the MainGame
class' IsFixedTimeStep to true and the TargetElapsedTime to 0.02, as
shown here in the Program.cs file:

```
game.IsFixedTimeStep = true;
game.TargetElapsedTime = TimeSpan.FromSeconds(1.0f / 50);
```

Setting IsFixedTimeStep to false will cause MonoGame to call the
Update() and Draw() methods without pausing in between, which could
yield 2,000 FPS, unless SynchronizeWithVerticalRetrace is set to true, in
which case the game's FPS will match the monitor's refresh rate.

The authors of the game you are diving into right now found that
turning off the vertical synchronization with the monitor and forcing
the game to run at 60 FPS made the game run much smoother, even
though this risks the possibility of tearing on the screen. One drawback
to the game as it is written currently is that all the game object velocities
are assuming that the game runs at 60 FPS. Go ahead and change the
FPS of the game and see how it behaves. Anything smaller than 60

and all the game objects, including the player's fighter jet, move much slower. Similarly, at higher FPS values, the game runs much faster! One improvement you will make to the game, given that you'd like to be able to run the game at different FPS values, is to use the GameTime object in your velocity calculations. For example, instead of assuming 60 FPS and having a PlayerSprite PlayerHorizontalSpeed of 10.0 per frame, you should set the velocity in units per seconds, so 600 units per second (10.0 times 60). Then in your movement calculations you move by 600 * gameTime.ElapsedGameTime.TotalSeconds. This should ensure that the plane moves at the same speed at 30 FPS or at 120 FPS.

Using Object Pools

One of the biggest potential contributors to a degradation in game performance is the garbage collector, which will run when the .Net Framework decides it makes sense to free up some memory and clean up objects that are not being referenced anymore. This collection of unused objects could happen very often, or not at all, depending on how the program is designed. The more often it runs, the more it can affect the game's performance by using up CPU time that should instead be spent on executing the Update() method.

One technique to avoid the garbage collector from running is to make sure your objects are always referenced by another object in the game. For example, when bullets fly off the screen and are not needed anymore, you could add them to a list of inactive objects. Because they are still referenced by the inactive list, they would not cause the garbage collector to run to clean them out from memory. However, this tactic is not a good solution. The list of inactive objects would keep growing over time. In a bullet hell type of game, there would be thousands of bullets created and then stored in the list, causing memory usage to grow infinitely.

17

Instead, you should find a way to reuse inactive objects. As bullets are needed by the game you could look at your list of inactive bullets and see if there are some available, reset their variables and properties, and reuse them. You would basically use refurbished bullets! You could also precreate bullets. If you knew how many bullets would be needed at one time, you could create that many bullets and immediately put them in the list of inactive objects, ready to be reused by the game. This technique is called pooling, except that the list of inactive objects is instead called a pool.

Let's implement a generic pool for your game objects for the game's engine:

```
public class GameObjectPool<T> where T : BaseGameObject
{
    private LinkedList<T> _activePool = new LinkedList<T>();
    private LinkedList<T> _inactivePool = new LinkedList<T>();
}
```

The GameObjectPool is of type T, where T must be a BaseGameObject. This means you'll be able to create pools of BulletSprite objects, or any other class instance that inherits from BaseGameObject. The pool has two lists: an active list and an inactive list. The strategy in this class is to shuffle objects between the two lists. Notice that the lists are linked lists. This is because inserting and removing objects from a linked list is an extremely fast operation. Let's look at the rest of the class, one element at a time.

```
public List<T> ActiveObjects
{
    get
    {
        var list = new List<T>();
        foreach (var gameObject in _activePool)
        {
            list.Add(gameObject);
        }
```

18

```
        return list;
    }
}
```

Accessing the ActiveObjects property will take the elements of the linked list and copy them into a list that is then returned.

```
public T GetOrCreate(Func<T> createNbObjectFn)
{
    T activatedObject;

    if (_inactivePool.Count > 0)
    {
        var gameObject = _inactivePool.First.Value;
        gameObject.Initialize();
        gameObject.Activate();
        activatedObject = gameObject;

        _activePool.AddLast(gameObject);
        _inactivePool.RemoveFirst();
    }
    else
    {
        var gameObject = createNbObjectFn();
        gameObject.Activate();
        activatedObject = gameObject;

        _activePool.AddLast(gameObject);
    }

    return activatedObject;
```

The GetOrCreate() function is called when a new object is needed by the game. It will look at the inactive list to first see if an unused object is available. If there is one, it will remove it from the inactive list, reinitialize it, call its Activate() method, add it to the list of active objects, and return it. If there are no objects available, then it will need to instantiate it. However, because the function does not know how to instantiate an object of type T, it must use a lambda function passed by the caller, which will return a new instance of the needed type. That new object is then activated and added to the list of active objects before being finally returned.

```
public void DeactivateObject(T gameObject, Action<T>
postDeactivateFn)
{
    var activeObject = _activePool.Find(gameObject);
    if (activeObject != null)
    {
        gameObject.Deactivate();

        _activePool.Remove(gameObject);
        _inactivePool.AddLast(gameObject);
    }

    postDeactivateFn(gameObject);
}
```

The DeactivateObject method is used when an object is no longer needed by the game. It takes as a parameter the object that needs to be discarded and a lambda to be called in case any post-deactivation steps need to be executed by the game. First, the code looks for the object in the list of active objects. If it is found, then the object is deactivated, removed from the list of active objects, and added to the inactive pool. Finally, the post-deactivation lambda is called.

Finally, you have a few life-quality methods to make everything a bit easier to call.

```
public void DeactivateObject(T gameObject)
{
    DeactivateObject(gameObject, _ => { });
}

public void DeactivateAllObjects(Action<T> postDeactivateFn)
{
    foreach (var gameObject in ActiveObjects)
    {
        DeactivateObject(gameObject, postDeactivateFn);
    }
}

public void DeactivateAllObjects()
{
    foreach (var gameObject in ActiveObjects)
    {
        DeactivateObject(gameObject);
    }
}
```

With your GameObjectPool in place, you can now use it to pool the game's bullets and avoid triggering a garbage collection run. In the GameplayState class, the code below accomplishes this.

First, the bullet list is updated to be a game object pool:

```
private GameObjectPool<BulletSprite> _bulletList =
    new GameObjectPool<BulletSprite>();
```

Further down, the game creates bullets using the code below. Most of the code is similar to the older version of this method, with the key distinction that you call the bullet pool's GetOrCreate() function, passing in a lambda that knows how to create new BulletSprite objects in case the bullet pool runs out of inactive bullets to reuse. It is interesting to note that adding objects to the game, or removing them from the game as you will see later, is not something the GameObjectPool is responsible for.

```
private void CreateBullets()
{
    var bulletY = _playerSprite.Position.Y + 30;
    var bulletLeftX = _playerSprite.Position.X + _playerSprite.
    Width / 2 - 40;

    var bulletRightX = _playerSprite.Position.X + _
    playerSprite.Width / 2 + 10;

    var bullet1 = _bulletList.GetOrCreate(() => new
    BulletSprite(_bulletTexture));
    var bullet2 = _bulletList.GetOrCreate(() => new
    BulletSprite(_bulletTexture));

    bullet1.Position = new Vector2(bulletLeftX, bulletY);
    bullet2.Position = new Vector2(bulletRightX, bulletY);

    AddGameObject(bullet1);
    AddGameObject(bullet2);
}
```

Then, the UpdateGameState() method is updated to only update active bullets from the pool:

```
public override void UpdateGameState(GameTime gameTime)
{
    foreach (var bullet in _bulletList.ActiveObjects)
    {
        bullet.MoveUp();
    }
}
```

In the code below, the DetectCollisions() method uses active bullets in its calculations and when a bullet hits another object, the object is deactivated and then removed from the game.

```
private void DetectCollisions()
{
    var bulletCollisionDetector =
        new AABBCollisionDetector<BulletSprite, BaseGameObject>
            (_bulletList.ActiveObjects);

    bulletCollisionDetector.DetectCollisions(
        _enemyList.ActiveObjects, (bullet, chopper) =>
    {
        _bulletList.DeactivateObject(bullet,
            b => RemoveGameObject(b));
    });
}
```

When the game is reset, after the player dies, then all bullets are deactivated at once:

```
private void ResetGame()
{
    _bulletList.DeactivateAllObjects(obj =>
    RemoveGameObject(obj));
}
```

Conclusion

In this chapter, you looked at why game performance is something that should be considered early in the creation of a game. You looked at FPS as a unit of measurement of game performance and what can happen when your game logic cannot be completed in the desired time frame, causing frames to be skipped. You also explored the relationship between frames per second and the computer monitor's Hertz rate. Finally, you discussed how to create an object pool to minimize the chance of triggering the garbage collector, one of the big culprits in decreased game performance.

There are other ways to improve game performance that we will not discuss in this book. Just to mention one other technique, a game does not have to perform all of the Update logic at every `Update()` call, like you are doing right now. While taking in player input and moving objects on the screen should happen as often as possible, AI agents or networking code do not have to be executing sixty times per second. Imagine an enemy object trying to find a path through debris. Once a path is found, it could only be updated four times per second instead of sixty.

This was your first stab at improving the game referenced at the beginning of this chapter. Your next step will be to extend the Content Pipeline Tool so that your levels are read as assets instead of embedded resources built with the source code.

CHAPTER 2

The Content Pipeline Tool

Sometimes improving a game concept means improving some of the structural components of the game, which may not yield any visual improvements. For example, if you want artists to contribute to the game and create 2D animations to embellish the game, it would save everyone some time if the artists could define each animation frame's position and dimensions on the sprite sheet. As it is right now, that information is defined in the code, so modifying a sprite sheet may require code changes. If you moved the animation details into the Content Pipeline Tool, artists would then be able to change animations without changing any code.

Note As in Chapter 1, you will keep improving the game developed in the *MonoGame Mastery* book.

In this chapter, you will learn

- How to extend the Content Pipeline Tool to handle custom assets

- How to migrating the player's animation into an asset managed by the Pipeline Tool

- How to add text translations to the game

© Louis Salin and Rami Morrar 2022
L. Salin and R. Morrar, *Game Development with MonoGame*,
https://doi.org/10.1007/978-1-4842-7771-3_2

The Content Pipeline Tool

First, let's start with a quick recap of what the Content Pipeline tool does for us. Its main utility to MonoGame developers is preprocessing assets so they are ready to be used in a game. It takes assets produced by graphic artists, musicians, level designers, and even programmers and transforms them so they can be used by the game code without needing to be processed again, even as the code changes and is recompiled. Once transformed, an asset does not need to be transformed again and is saved to disk in its new, transformed state as an .xnb file. As a bonus, it is also compressed to take up less space.

The content pipeline performs its work in four individual steps. It first calls an importer object that will load the asset from disk into memory. Then a processor is invoked, which transforms the data in memory into a data structure that is usable by the game. Finally, because you do not want to reprocess the asset when the game runs, the pipeline will store the data structure back to disk as an .xnb file using a writer object. When the game is launched and the asset is needed, a reader object will be called internally by MonoGame to load the data structure as-is so it can be used immediately without further transformations. Figure 2-1 shows this process for a .png image asset, which can be transformed into a Texture2D object by the pipeline.

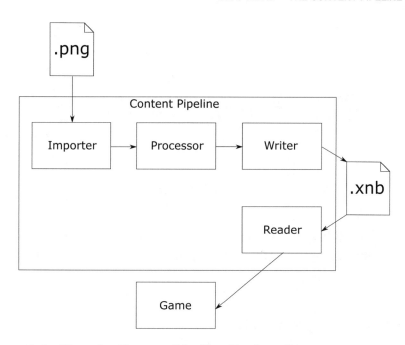

Figure 2-1. *How the Content Pipeline Tool works*

There are two ways to kick off the Content Pipeline Tool. One is from within its graphical user interface. The other is from Visual Studio when the project is built. When creating new MonoGame projects using the available Visual Studio templates, a Content.mgcb file will be generated and included in the project in the Content directory of the project. When right-clicking on that file and selecting its properties, you can see what is shown in Figure 2-2. Content.mgcb has a custom build action called MonoGameContentReference which will invoke the Content Pipeline Tool to process all of the assets as part of compiling the code. That build action is defined in the installed MonoGame NuGet package, located in the .nuget folder in your home directory. For example, mine is in C:\Users\LouisSalin\.nuget\packages\monogame.content.builder. task\3.8.0.1641\build\MonoGame.Content.Builder.Task.targets.

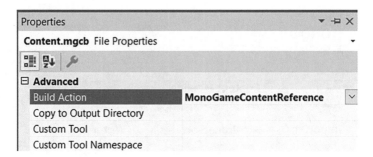

Figure 2-2. *The Content.mgcb build action*

Let's look at the four types of objects needed by the content pipeline individually and look at how an image is imported and processed into a Texture2D object by the pipeline.

The Content Importer

The Content Importer is a class that is used to load an asset from disk. The class must inherit from ContentImporter<T> and be marked by a ContentImporter attribute. This will allow the Content Pipeline Tool to discover the importer and present it as an option in the Importer drop-down. Figure 2-3 shows the available importers in the Content Pipeline Tool, with the Texture Importer selected.

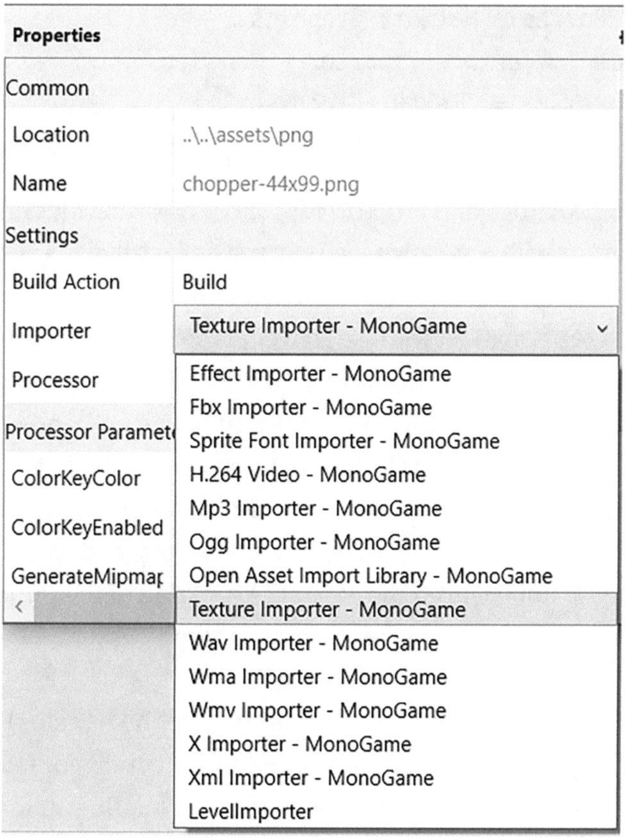

Figure 2-3. *The list of importers available in the Content Pipeline Tool*

Within the MonoGame framework, the Texture Importer is defined like this:

```
[ContentImporter(
 ".bmp", // Bitmap Image File
 // ... there are a lot of image file types defined, most of which
 // ... was edited out for reading purposes
 ".jng", ".jpg", ".jpeg", ".jpe", ".jif", ".jfif", ".jfi",
 // JPEG
```

```
".png", //Portable Network Graphics
DisplayName = "Texture Importer - MonoGame",
DefaultProcessor = "TextureProcessor")]
public class TextureImporter : ContentImporter<TextureContent>
```

The code above declares a TextureImporter class that inherits from the ContentImporter with a generic type TextureContent that is a class type that will be used to hold the image data in memory once the asset is loaded. The TextureImporter is marked with the ContentImporter class attribute that defines which file types can be imported by this code, which display name to put in the drop-down selection of the content pipeline tool, and which content processor class will be needed to process the asset once loaded.

The importer's job is simple: open up a file stream, read the content of the file, and store the data into an instance of an object designed to hold that data. This is done within the Import() function of the importer. Once loaded, the content pipeline takes the data and passes it to the next stage of the pipeline, where it will be processed.

You will keep looking at how the content pipeline handles textures in this section, so it is important to note that the TextureImporter actually creates an instance of a Texture2DContent when loading an image, which is fine because Texture2DContent inherits from TextureContent, used as the generic type of the importer. This will be important to remember later.

The Content Processor

Similarly to the importer above, the content processor is also selectable from a drop-down in the Content Pipeline Tool, as Figure 2-4 shows. The processors available to the Pipeline Tool must inherit from the ContentProcessor<TInput, TOutput> abstract class and be marked by a ContentProcessor attribute that is used to specify the display name of the processor in the drop-down. The idea behind the processor is to take an object of type TInput and transform it into an object of type TOutput before passing it onto the next stage of the pipeline.

Let's keep looking at how your images are processed into textures. The **TextureProcessor** is defined like this:

```
[ContentProcessor(DisplayName="Texture - MonoGame")]
public class TextureProcessor : ContentProcessor<Texture
Content, TextureContent>
```

Here, the TextureProcessor class is designed to transform an object of type TextureContent into a new object of the same type. Since the importer you looked at above creates Texture2DContent objects, which inherit from TextureContent, the output of the TextureProcessor is also a Texture2DContent instance. One of the things that is done by the processor is the generation of mipmaps, if they are needed.

Content processors can have parameters that are displayed under the Processor Parameters section of the Content Pipeline Tool's properties. Those parameters are read from the content processor class. Any class property in the content processor class with a public getter and setter will be shown by the Content Pipeline Tool and the user will be able to change their values. Figure 2-4 happens to show the processor parameters made available by the TextureProcessor:

- ColorKeyColor

- ColorKeyEnabled

- GenerateMipmaps

- PremultiplyAlpha

- MakeSquare

- ResizeToPowerOfTwo

- TextureFormat

31

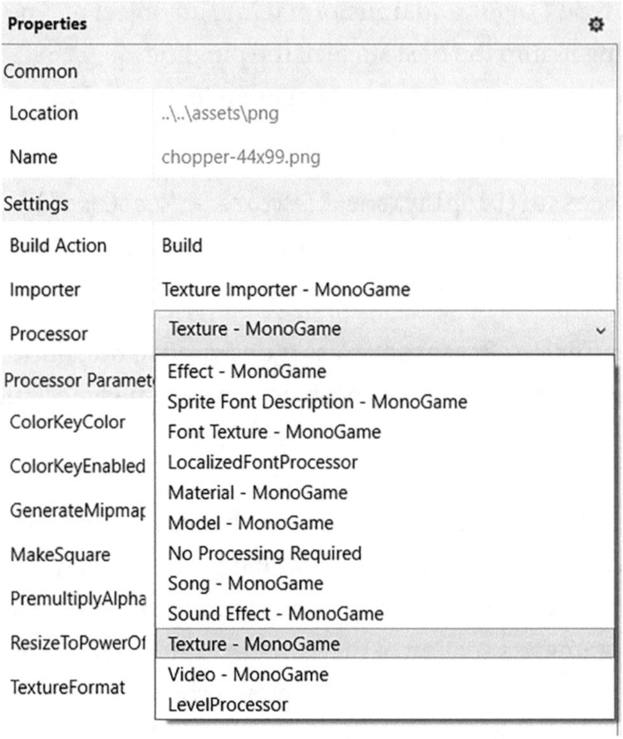

Figure 2-4. *The list of processors available in the Content Pipeline Tool and available processor parameters*

The processor parameters can be marked with a DefaultValueAttribute if you desire to change their default values, which is based on the type of the parameter.

Let's look at how the TextureProcessor defined all these parameters:

```
[DefaultValueAttribute(typeof(Color), "255,0,255,255")]
public virtual Color ColorKeyColor { get; set; }
[DefaultValueAttribute(true)]
public virtual bool ColorKeyEnabled { get; set; }
public virtual bool GenerateMipmaps { get; set; }
[DefaultValueAttribute(true)]
```

```
public virtual bool PremultiplyAlpha { get; set; }
public virtual bool ResizeToPowerOfTwo { get; set; }
public virtual bool MakeSquare { get; set; }
public virtual TextureProcessorOutputFormat TextureFormat {
get; set; }
```

Now that you have imported and processed your textures, it is time to save them back to disk.

The Content Writer

Saving a processed asset back to disk in an `.xnb` format is the job of the content writer. Content writers are discovered at runtime by the content pipeline tool when the time comes to save processed data of a certain type, so in order to save data of a certain type, T, there must be a class in the codebase that inherits from `ContentTypeWriter<T>` and is marked by the `ContentTypeWriter` attribute. Without that, no writer class will be found and the Pipeline Tool will fail to generate an `.xnb` file.

Let's take a look at how the pipeline saves instances of the `Texture2DContent` class to an `.xnb` file. Within the framework, there is a class defined that satisfies your conditions for a valid content writer:

```
[ContentTypeWriter]
class Texture2DWriter : BuiltInContentWriter<Texture2DContent>
```

Note that `BuiltInContentWriter<T>` inherits from `ContentTypeWriter<T>`, so this works. The `BuiltInContentWriter` class is private and is only used for the content types that are built into the framework.

The `Write()` method of a given content writer will be called by the pipeline tool with two parameters: an output object with an interface allowing its user to write many different kinds of values to disk as binary data, and the content object that needs to be saved.

33

One secondary aspect of the content writer is that it is also responsible for indicating which content reader will be needed to load the .xnb file back into memory. Once the content object has been serialized, the Flush() method is called on the output object by the pipeline. This will cause a header to be written near the start of the .xnb file, and one of the elements in the header is the full class name of the content reader that will be instantiated to load the data back from disk. The name is accessed by calling the GetRuntimeReader() function on the content reader. You will not see one on the Texture2DWriter because it is overridden in its BuiltInContentWriter base class, where the content reader class name is set to the same name as the content writer (Texture2DWriter here), except that "Writer" is replaced with "Reader." Using that logic, loading a Texture2DContent object will require an instance of the Texture2DReader, which we will discuss next.

The Content Reader

The content reader is a class that must inherit from ContentTypeReader<T>. Contrary to the other three classes used by the Content Pipeline Tool, this class does not need to be marked by an attribute. This is because this class is not auto-discovered by the MonoGame framework. Instead, when loading an .xnb file from disk, one of the file headers has the full class name that needs to be used to load the file. Once the class name has been read from the file headers, MonoGame will create an instance of the class and call its Read() function, which will load the same binary data that was written to disk by the content writer. This is all done when the content manager's Load<T>() function is called to load an asset into the game.

Here is how the Texture2DReader is defined in the framework:

```
internal class Texture2DReader : ContentTypeReader<Texture2D>
```

You have finally come full circle. The `Texture2DReader` inherits from `ContentTypeReader` of type `Texture2D`, which is exactly what you want when call the `LoadTexture` in your game engine:

```
protected Texture2D LoadTexture(string textureName)
{
  return _contentManager.Load<Texture2D>(textureName);
}
```

To recap, an image is processed into a texture by going through the following steps:

- A `.png` file (or other supported file format) is loaded by the `TextureImporter`, which creates a `Texture2DContent` object.

- The `Texture2DContent` object is processed and enriched by the `TextureProcessor`.

- The enriched `Texture2DContent` object is then saved to an `.xnb` file by the `Texture2DWriter`, where one of the `.xnb` file headers is set to the full class name of the `Texture2DReader` class so it can be read from disk.

- Finally, the MonoGame reads an `.xnb` file, determines that a `Texture2DReader` instance is required, and uses it to read the file into a `Texture2D` object for the game.

We covered quite a bit of internal details here, but this knowledge will be important should you want to develop your own importers, processors, writers, and readers. Extending the content pipeline tool to be able to handle custom data types is not too unusual and it is something you can do right now.

Extending the Content Pipeline Tool

One improvement you can make to the game is to extract the level text files from the solution, where `Levels\LevelData\level1.txt` is currently set as an embedded resource, and instead treat them as game assets. This allows level designers to contribute to the game without having to open the code and compile it whenever they make a change. They instead only need to open the text files in their favorite text editor, edit the levels, and then run the Content Pipeline Tool.

But because the content pipeline does not know how to turn a level text file into a Level object that can be used by the game, you need to teach it how to use the `LevelReader` to create an instance of a Level object.

To quickly recap how levels are loaded in the game, the `LevelReader` reads the text file, which is a grid of comma-separated numbers where a **0** indicates an empty tile and a **1** indicates the presence of a shooting turret. The last element at the end of every row represents an event. An underscore means nothing happens and a letter g followed by a number tells the game to generate that many numbers of choppers. It is very simplistic and will be improved upon in Chapter 4. For now, you will concentrate on making the level text files assets managed by the pipeline.

As you saw earlier, to create your own pipeline extension, you need to create a level importer, a level processor, a level writer, and a level reader. Once they are compiled into a library DLL, you tell the Content Pipeline Tool to reference that DLL and it will be able to scan it and offer you the new importer and processor.

Creating a Pipeline Extension

MonoGame has a template for creating pipeline extensions. In Visual Studio, create a new project and select the MonoGame Pipeline Extension template, as shown in Figure 2-5. Name your project **PipelineExtensions**.

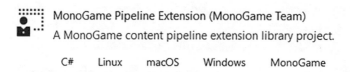

MonoGame Pipeline Extension (MonoGame Team)

A MonoGame content pipeline extension library project.

C#   Linux   macOS   Windows   MonoGame

Figure 2-5. *The MonoGame Pipeline Extension template*

This will create a .Net 2.0 C# library project in your solution that contains two initial files: `Importer1.cs` and `Processor1.cs`. Before compiling the project, set it up in the solution to be compiled in Release mode, as seen in Figure 2-6. To configure solution properties, right-click the solution and click Properties.

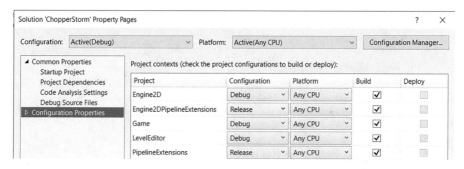

Figure 2-6. *Setting your pipeline extension projects to be built in release mode*

Compile the solution and then open the Content Pipeline Tool application. Click the top level Content item in the asset tree view to look at its properties. One of them, all the way at the bottom, is the list of references imported into the tool. It should look like Figure 2-7.

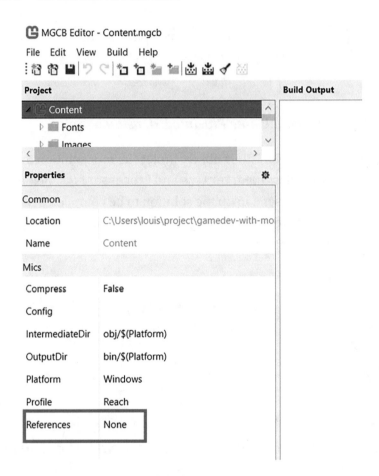

Figure 2-7. *The properties of the Content root item*

Click the References property and a pop-up will open, as shown in Figure 2-8. Click the Add button and navigate to where your pipeline extension project's DLL is being built. It should be in the `PipelineExtensions\bin\Release\netstandard2.0\` folder. Select the `PipelineeExtensions.DLL` file and click Okay to close the pop-up.

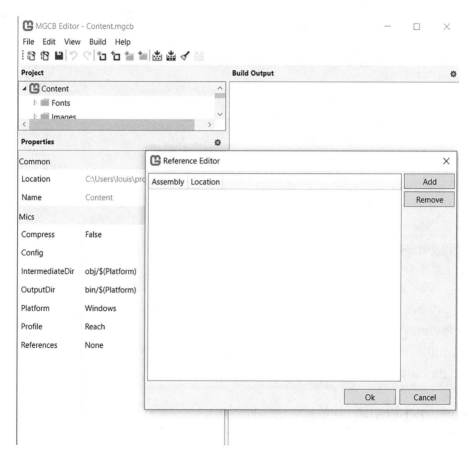

Figure 2-8. *Adding references to the Content Pipeline Tool*

You should now see Importer1 and Processor1 in the drop-down options when selecting processors and importers for your assets. See Figure 2-9 for an example.

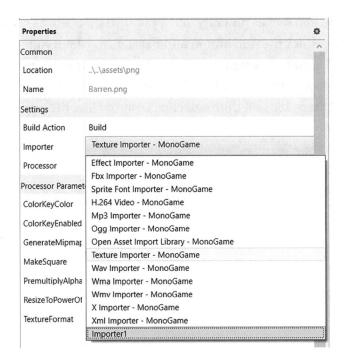

Figure 2-9. *Importer1 is now an option*

Note that from this point on, you will need to close the Content Pipeline Tool application when you make changes to the **PipelineExtensions** project because it is using its DLL file and Visual Studio will not be able to overwrite it. Close it now since you are about to make changes.

Adding Logic to Your Extension

Let's create your four pipeline building blocks. First, delete `Importer1. cs` and `Processor1.cs`. These two files will not be necessary anymore. Instead, create these four classes:

- `LevelImporter`

- `LevelProcessor`

- LevelWriter

- LevelReader

Your level importer will read the level text files and transform them into a single string. Then your level processor will take in the string and output a Level object that will be saved as an .xnb file by the level writer. Finally, the level reader will be in charge of reading in the .xnb level file and giving your game a Level object to work with.

This will change how the game code accesses and interacts with level assets. While we will not cover this part of the code in this chapter, please refer to the book's source code for the full details of how the game code was modified to accommodate the new pipeline extensions. We will only go over the extension's code in this chapter. It suffices to say that the responsibilities of reading in a level text file as a string and transforming it to a list of level events has been moved to the pipeline extension project in the Level.cs file.

Loading and Saving Assets

With that said, let's take a look at your LevelImporter class:

```
[ContentImporter(".txt", DisplayName = "LevelImporter",
 DefaultProcessor = "LevelProcessor")]
public class LevelImporter : ContentImporter<string>
{
 public override string Import(string filename,
 ContentImporterContext context)
 {
 return File.ReadAllText(filename);
 }
}
```

The class inherits from `ContentImporter<string>`, meaning it will load the asset file and output a string. It is also marked with the `ContentImporter` attribute, which specifies that level asset files will be .txt files, that the Content Pipeline Tool application will use the name **LevelImporter** in the drop-down options and that the pipeline will pass the output string to the `LevelProcessor` class.

You then override the `Import()` function and use the basic `IO.File.ReadAllText()` function to read the entire .txt file, referenced by the filename parameter provided to you by the content pipeline when it calls your extension, as a string.

While you do not use the context parameter here, it can be useful for debugging purposes. Its properties can be used to inspect the intermediate and output directories of the current processor and the `Logger` property provides a logger that you can use to output messages while running the Content Pipeline Tool.

Next, your `LevelProcessor` will look like this:

```
[ContentProcessor(DisplayName = "LevelProcessor")]
public class LevelProcessor : ContentProcessor<string, Level>
{
  public override Level Process(string input,
  ContentProcessorContext context)
  {
  return new Level(input);
  }
}
```

The `LevelProcessor` inherits from `ContentProcessor<string, Level>`, which means that its overridden `Process()` function takes a string as input and will output a Level object. It is also marked by the `ContentProcessor` attribute with a `DisplayName` of **LevelProcessor**. Note that in the book's source code, there is a `Level` class in the

PipelineExtensions project and this is what the code is referring to here, not the Game's Level class. The process of transforming a string into a Level is described in detail in the *MonoGame Mastery* book and its code has been migrated into the extension's Level class.

Now let's take a look at your LevelWriter so you can create the .xnb files, which will simply output the level as a string, the same string that was read from the original asset file. You could have been more precise and output the level grid's dimensions, followed by each value of each row, but saving the string itself is more flexible at this point given that you will change the level assets in Chapter 4.

```
[ContentTypeWriter]
public class LevelWriter : ContentTypeWriter<Level>
{
  public override string GetRuntimeReader(TargetPlatform
  targetPlatform)
  {
  return "PipelineExtensions.LevelReader, PipelineExtensions";
  }

  protected override void Write(ContentWriter output, Level
  value)
  {
  output.Write(value.LevelStringEncoding);
  }
}
```

The LevelWriter is discovered by the content pipeline when the time comes to save the processed output into an .xnb file, because it is marked by the ContentTypeWriter attribute. A lot of work is done for you by the framework at this point, like creating the .xnb file and writing its headers. All you need to provide here is an overridden GetRuntimeReader()

function that returns the full class name of the LevelReader class that will be used to read the .xnb file back, and an overridden Write() method that you can use to write the Level value to disk as a binary file.

Finally, here is your LevelReader class:

```
public class LevelReader : ContentTypeReader<Level>
{
 protected override Level Read(ContentReader input, Level
 existingInstance)
 {
 return new Level(input.ReadString());
 }
}
```

The LevelReader inherits from ContentTypeReader<Level>, which indicates that its Read() function will return an instance of the Level class. Read() takes two parameters: a ContentReader object that knows how to read different binary values and convert them into basic types, and an existingInstance of the object you are trying to create, which can be confusing. Before calling the Read() function, the pipeline will create a default instance of the desired object and pass it in as the existingInstance. Here, you are ignoring the parameter and creating a new instance of the level yourself.

Now that your pieces are in place, you can move your level files out of the code base and treat them just like any other asset. In the books' source code, the evel1.txt file was moved to assets\levels\level1.txt alongside the sounds, music, and texture assets. It was then added to the Content Pipeline Tool into the Levels folder, as shown in Figure 2-10.

Figure 2-10. *level1.txt is now an asset*

Adding Animations to the Content Pipeline

Animations are another thing that can be moved out of the code and given to the Content Pipeline Tool to manage. The game already has animation sprite sheets managed as assets, but the details of the animation are in the code, which specifies each animation cell's position, dimensions, and lifespan. In the original game, the PlayerSprite's animations are defined in code as follows:

```
Animation _turnRightAnimation = new Animation(false);

_turnLeftAnimation.AddFrame(
 new Rectangle(348, 0, AnimationCellWidth,
AnimationCellHeight),
 AnimationSpeed);
_turnLeftAnimation.AddFrame(
 new Rectangle(232, 0, AnimationCellWidth,
AnimationCellHeight),
 AnimationSpeed);
_turnLeftAnimation.AddFrame(
 new Rectangle(116, 0, AnimationCellWidth,
AnimationCellHeight),
 AnimationSpeed);
_turnLeftAnimation.AddFrame(
 new Rectangle(0, 0, AnimationCellWidth, AnimationCellHeight),
 AnimationSpeed);
```

Each animation only has four frames to define but specifying all of this in code for more complex animations with more frames will get cumbersome very quickly. Instead, you could move all that information into an XML file that lives as an asset right next to its associated sprite sheet asset. While you could store that information in a different format, like JSON or YAML, the Content Pipeline Tool comes with a built-in XML importer that you can use and thus avoid building another extension.

Before you build the XML asset, however, you define the data structure that will store the animation data in the code and then use it to create your XML file. This data structure must be referenced by the Content Pipeline Tool so it can access it. When it parses the XML file, it will instantiate it and populate its public properties automatically for you. This means the data structure must be in a library whose DLL is referenced by the Content pipeline Tool, similarly to what you did earlier.

You could add a new class to your **PipelineExtensions** project since it is already being referenced, but you would miss the opportunity to improve your game engine. Animations are already part of the engine and defining animation cell positions, dimensions, and lifespans should belong to the engine. So, the engine also needs a reference to your data structure. The only way to gracefully handle this scenario is to create a new MonoGame **PipelineExtension** project in your solution that will strictly be used by the engine and not your game. Go ahead and create the project as you did in the previous section and name it **Engine2DPipelineExtensions**. One day, when the engine is ready to be separated from the game into its own library, it will come with its own sets of pipeline extensions, which will include the ability to read animation data from an XML file.

In the new project, create a new class named `AnimationData.cs`:

```
public class AnimationData
{
 public int AnimationSpeed;
 public bool IsLooping;
 public List<AnimationFrameData> Frames;
}

public class AnimationFrameData
{
 public int X;
 public int Y;
 public int CellWidth;
 public int CellHeight;
}
```

The data structure above mimics what you see in the code. First, an animation is created with a flag that indicates if it is a looping animation or not. You also add the animation speed at the animation level instead of in the frames because animations tend to use the same speed for all their frames. Then you have a list of animation frame data that includes its position on the sprite sheet and its dimensions.

When the XML asset is read, it will create an `AnimationData` object that will include all the frames needed to perform the animation. But what will this XML look like and how do you create it? One quick trick you can use is to write code that creates an `AnimationData` object and saves it as XML, and then use the resulting XML file as your template to build the asset.

Creating the XML Template

`Program.cs` is the piece of code that starts your game, so let's temporarily generate your XML template there. First, install the `MonoGame.Framework.Content.Pipeline` to the Game project. It will be used to serialize your `AnimationData` object into an XML file. Then, open `Program.cs` and add the following code at the beginning of the `Main()` method. Remember, this is all temporary. Once you have your XML template, you will undo all of this.

```
// using Microsoft.Xna.Framework.Content.Pipeline.
Serialization.Intermediate;
// using System.Xml;

AnimationData data = new AnimationData();
AnimationFrameData frame1 = new AnimationFrameData();
AnimationFrameData frame2 = new AnimationFrameData();

frame1.X = 1;
frame1.Y = 1;
frame1.CellHeight = 1;
frame1.CellWidth = 1;
```

```
frame2.X = 2;
frame2.Y = 2;
frame2.CellHeight = 2;
frame2.CellWidth = 2;

data.AnimationSpeed = 1;
data.IsLooping = true;
data.Frames = new System.Collections.Generic.
List<AnimationFrameData> {
 frame1, frame2 };

XmlWriterSettings settings = new XmlWriterSettings();
settings.Indent = true;

using (XmlWriter writer = XmlWriter.Create("animation.xml",
settings))
{
 IntermediateSerializer.Serialize(writer, data, null);
}
```

This code starts with two comments that indicate which namespaces need to be imported into the code if you are not using Visual Studio to auto-discover them.

Here you start by creating a simple `AnimationData` object with dummy data. Then you use an `XmlWriter` and the content pipeline's serializer to transform that data to an XML file. When you run the game, it will generate the template XML file for you before loading the game. All you need to do now is go fetch that XML file and delete all the code you just wrote. The file, located in `Game\bin\Debug\net5.0` (or somewhere equivalent depending on which .Net version you are using), will look like this:

```
<?xml version="1.0" encoding="utf-8"?>
<XnaContent xmlns:PipelineExtensions="Engine2D.
PipelineExtensions">
```

```
<Asset Type="PipelineExtensions:AnimationData">
<AnimationSpeed>1</AnimationSpeed>
<IsLooping>true</IsLooping>
<Frames>
<Item>
<X>1</X>
<Y>1</Y>
<CellWidth>1</CellWidth>
<CellHeight>1</CellHeight>
</Item>
<Item>
<X>2</X>
<Y>2</Y>
<CellWidth>2</CellWidth>
<CellHeight>2</CellHeight>
</Item>
</Frames>
</Asset>
</XnaContent>
```

The XML file starts with an XnaContent tag that indicates which
assembly contains the class that you want to write the data to. It is followed
by an Asset tag that is used to map the data below with a specific class
that will receive it. From there, each tag represents a public variable on
the class and lists, like the Frames list, contain a series of Item tags that are
used to fill each frame in the list. With this information, you can move your
PlayerSprite animation data into an asset.

Creating the TurnLeft Animation Asset

Create a new file named turn_left.xml in the assets\animations\ Player folder:

```xml
<?xml version="1.0" encoding="utf-8"?>
<XnaContent xmlns:PipelineExtensions="Engine2D.
PipelineExtensions">
 <Asset Type="PipelineExtensions:AnimationData">
 <AnimationSpeed>3</AnimationSpeed>
 <IsLooping>false</IsLooping>
 <Frames>
 <Item>
 <X>348</X>
 <Y>0</Y>
 <CellWidth>116</CellWidth>
 <CellHeight>152</CellHeight>
 </Item>
 <Item>
 <X>232</X>
 <Y>0</Y>
 <CellWidth>116</CellWidth>
 <CellHeight>152</CellHeight>
 </Item>
 <Item>
 <X>116</X>
 <Y>0</Y>
 <CellWidth>116</CellWidth>
 <CellHeight>152</CellHeight>
 </Item>
 <Item>
 <X>0</X>
 <Y>0</Y>
```

```
 <CellWidth>116</CellWidth>
 <CellHeight>152</CellHeight>
 </Item>
 </Frames>
 </Asset>
</XnaContent>
```

This file follows the same format as your template, but is filled with the data used in original game code used to create the `_turnLeftAnimation` animation. Now add this file to the content pipeline tool, set the importer to the "Xml Importer – MonoGame," the processor to "No Processing Required," and build the assets, which should build the `.xnb` file for the animation. All that you need to do now is load it as game content and build the animation from the `AnimationData` object.

Add a new function to load your `AnimationData` to the `BaseGameState` class:

```
protected AnimationData LoadAnimation(string animationName)
{
 return _contentManager.Load<AnimationData>(animationName);
}
```

Add the following private constant to the `GameplayState` class:

```
private const string PlayerAnimationTurnLeft =
 "Sprites/Animations/FighterSpriteTurnLeft";
```

Then load the animation by calling and pass it to the `PlayerSprite` object via a new constructor parameter:

```
var turnLeftAnimation = _contentManager.Load<AnimationData>
(animationName);
```

```
public PlayerSprite(Texture2D texture, AnimationData
turnLeftAnimation)
  : base(texture)
{
 // ... code edited out
 _turnLeftAnimation = new Animation(turnLeftAnimation);
}
```

Then you need to create a new Animation constructor that can be called with an AnimationData object:

```
public Animation(AnimationData data)
{
 _isLoop = data.IsLooping;
 foreach( var frame in data.Frames )
 {
 AddFrame(
 new Rectangle(frame.X, frame.Y, frame.CellWidth, frame.
 CellHeight),
 data.AnimationSpeed);
 }
}
```

Finally, after doing the same thing for the turnRightAnimation, running the game should give you the exact same behavior as the original game. While you have not improved the game itself, you have added flexibility into how you build your game assets and decoupled animation details from the code.

Internationalizing Game Text

The last thing you will tackle in this chapter is how to use the Content Pipeline Tool to automatically create SpriteFonts that can be used to draw text in any language. The game you are improving did not have any internationalization in place and the text displayed on the screen is only in English. You will improve on this in two steps:

- Use string resources for each language the game will support and let the .Net Framework localize your game appropriately.

- Use the Localized Font Processor to generate Unicode SpriteFonts.

The original game's Content Pipeline Tool only generates SpriteFonts for all the English characters when you build your assets. For each character of the English language, the content pipeline generates a texture that will be used to draw that character on the screen. But why not create textures for all existing Unicode characters? Because this would take a very long time. So, you need a different strategy that will build Unicode textures for only the characters that are used in the game. This is done by using the Localized Font Processor for your fonts, as seen in Figure 2-11. What this processor does is look at the SpriteFont XML file for the ResourceFiles tag, which lists all the .Net resource files you have in your project.

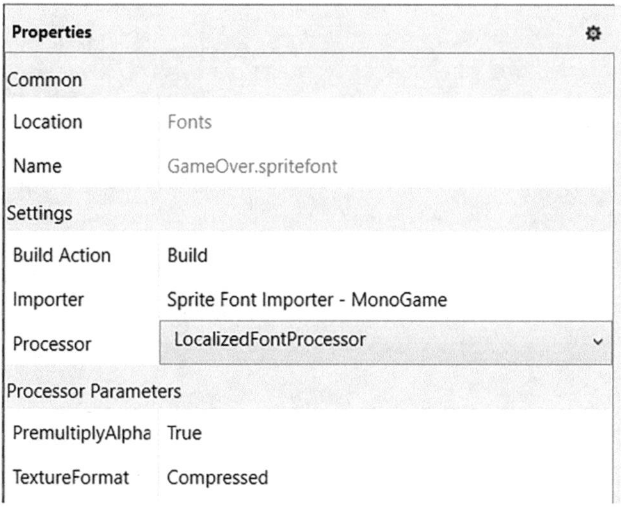

Properties		⚙
Common		
Location	Fonts	
Name	GameOver.spritefont	
Settings		
Build Action	Build	
Importer	Sprite Font Importer - MonoGame	
Processor	LocalizedFontProcessor	⌄
Processor Parameters		
PremultiplyAlpha	True	
TextureFormat	Compressed	

Figure 2-11. *Selecting the Localized Font Processor*

For each resource file, it looks at all the strings in the file and only creates textures for the characters in the string.

So, let's start by creating your resource files and getting the .Net localization system involved. As shown in Figure 2-12, right-click the Content folder in the Game project and add a new Resource item called Strings.resx1.

Figure 2-12. *Adding your first resource*

Once the resource has been added, double-click it and edit the resource file so that it has everything, as shown in Figure 2-13.

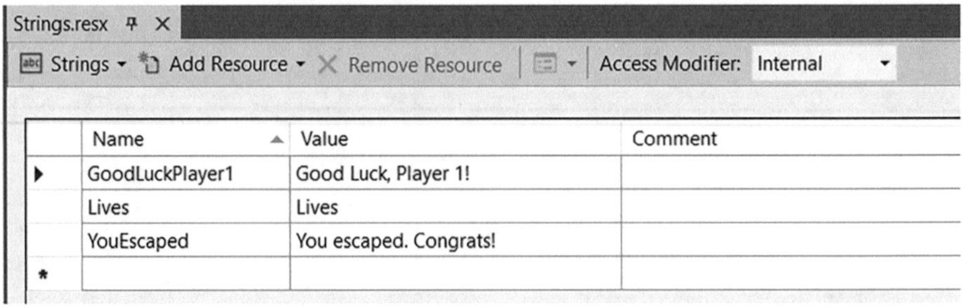

Figure 2-13. *English text*

You can see that this has all the text needed by the game so far. Now let's change the code to use this resource file instead of the hardcoded strings in the code. Replace any instance of the text in the resource file with the corresponding resource. For example, this line in `GameplayState.cs` changes from

```
_levelStartEndText.Text = "Good Luck, Player 1!";
```

to

```
_levelStartEndText.Text = Strings.GoodLuckPlayer1;
```

Then, edit `Program.cs` to add this to the start of the `Main()` method:

```
Strings.Culture = CultureInfo.CurrentCulture;
```

This sets the culture of the app to the current culture of the machine that is running the game.

You now need to add some text translations. Create two new resource files in the `Content` folder called

- `Strings.fr.resx`
- `Strings.ja.resx`

By using this format, the .Net Framework will automatically choose the right Strings resource file based on which culture is set for the game. The French and Japanese cultures are codified by the "fr" and "ja" codes, so if you set the game to those cultures, .Net will use the codes to find the right resource file. If a resource file is not found for a certain code, then .Net will default to the `Strings.resx` file, which uses English text.

See Figures 2-14 and 2-15 for the content of the resource files in French and Japanese. Please note that I do not speak Japanese, so I used Google Translate to get the Japanese strings.

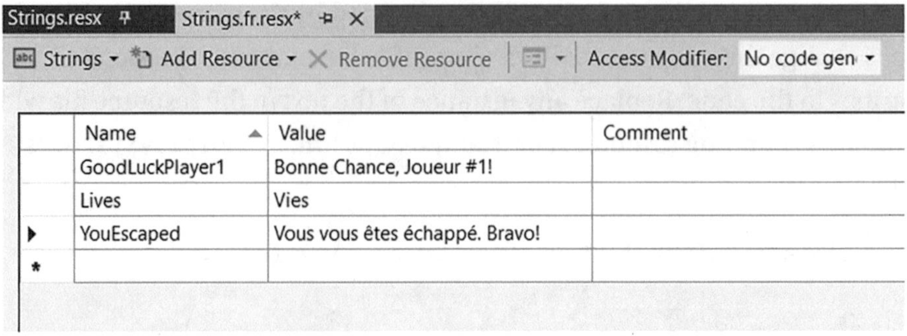

Figure 2-14. *French text*

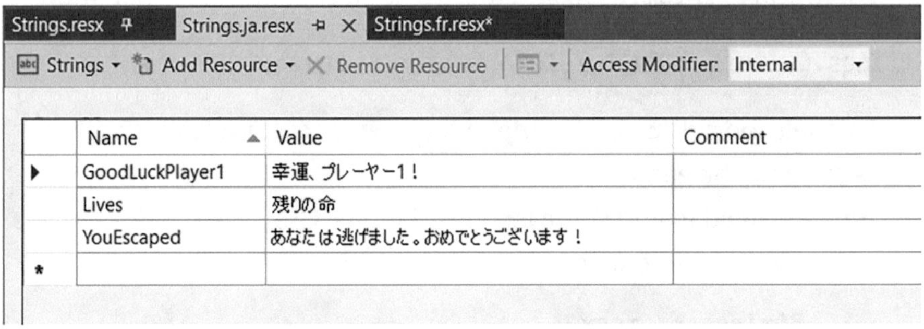

Figure 2-15. *Japanese text*

Now back in `Program.cs`, you can force the game to use the French or Japanese language by forcing the game culture to those languages, for example, by replacing the line of code that sets the current culture with this line:

```
Strings.Culture = CultureInfo.GetCultureInfo(JAPANESE);
```

Build and run the game and you will see that you have one more problem, however. Instead of Japanese characters, you have blank boxes, as seen in Figure 2-16.

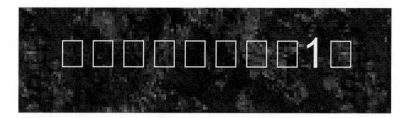

Figure 2-16. *Blank text fonts*

This is because you are using the Arial font, which, as installed on my Windows machine, does not have Japanese characters. When the Content Pipeline Tool builds the font textures, it rasterizes the font found on the builder's machine into a texture. But if the font does not have the desired characters, then a blank box is instead rendered into the texture.

The easiest solution is to change the font from Arial to MS Gothic in the SpriteFont files, which does include Japanese characters. Unfortunately, however, its English characters are not very pretty. So, a better solution is to download a better font from the Internet. The Noto Serif JP font is freely available here: https://fonts.google.com/specimen/Noto+Serif+JP. Download and install it, and then change the font from Arial in all the SpriteFonts in Game\Content\Fonts to this new font:

```
<FontName>Noto Serif JP</FontName>
```

Rebuild the project and you should see Japanese text, like in Figure 2-17.

Figure 2-17. *Japanese text correctly rendered on the screen*

Conclusion

In this chapter, you took a deep dive into the Content Pipeline Tool and how its four building blocks (the content importer, the content processor, the content writer, and the content reader) all work together to take an asset file and produce a reusable game asset. You then extended the Content Pipeline Tool so it can process level files and animation details as proper game assets. Finally, you set up your game to be translated into many different languages using the Localized Font Processor and resource strings.

CHAPTER 3

Cameras and Layers

There are a few improvements you can make to the game in terms of how you organize game objects into the game world. The game places objects directly on the screen by using screen coordinates to position objects and then simply renders the objects in place with no further transformation needed besides a simple scaling effect when some sprite objects are simply too big. While this works reasonably well for a simple game, it adds the complexity of bringing objects into the screen as the game evolves. The choppers and turrets, for example, must be spawned just off screen and then moved into position to create the illusion that the player is continuously moving up through the level. Furthermore, spawning objects off screen becomes more difficult if you add the ability to change the resolution at which your game is rendered. The $x = 1,500$ axis might be off screen if the screen resolution is 1280 x 720, but not if it is 1920 x 1080.

In the process of improving the game, you will also completely break it. In this chapter, you will

- Learn how cameras work and the possibilities they open up.

- Add a camera to the game.

- Create a new game state where the player and the camera constantly move up.

© Louis Salin and Rami Morrar 2022
L. Salin and R. Morrar, *Game Development with MonoGame*,
https://doi.org/10.1007/978-1-4842-7771-3_3

Cameras

One of the most drastic changes to a game is the addition of a camera as a way to view the game world from different angles and positions. Imagine being the director of a movie. You are outside, filming a busy street scene with people going about their business while the camera is rolled down the middle of the street, creating an interesting visual impact. In video games, the camera works in the same way. Game objects are placed in the world and the camera's job is to move around the game world and capture what it sees onto the screen. Instead of having shooting turrets artificially moving down the screen to create the illusion of movement, they will instead be fixed in place in the game world and the camera will move around with the player.

Your cameras are an abstraction, of course. They do not really "see" the world. Instead, they abstract over a series of transformations that are applied to all game objects as they are rendered to the screen. These transformations take the game object coordinates and dimensions in the game world and change them to the screen coordinates where the object will ultimately be drawn. Figure 3-1 shows the same game world as "seen" by a camera in two different positions and how that affects the position of the world's objects on the screen. As you can see, moving the camera around the game world causes different parts of the world to be drawn on the screen. Using camera A, only the bottom left portion of the house is drawn and the tree is completely ignored, while using camera B, located further back and moved a bit to the right, allows the entire scene to be drawn on the screen. All of this is accomplished without moving any game object.

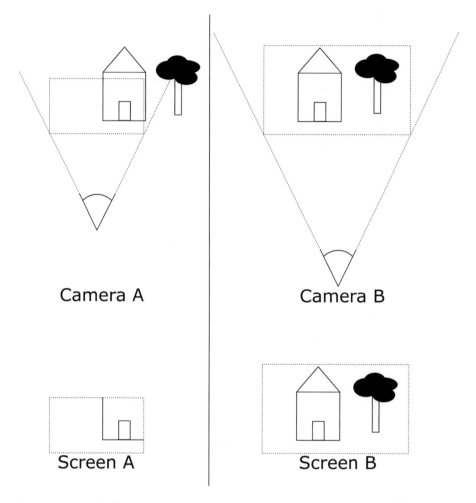

Figure 3-1. *Different camera placements show the world differently*

Using cameras in the game will open up a few possibilities and simplify things. One thing you will work on in a later chapter is building a level editor, where you can position turrets way off screen and use a camera to simulate gameplay. Without cameras, positioning turrets in the level designer would have to translate into spawning turrets when the player reaches the appropriate location, which is more complicated and prone to bugs.

How Cameras Work

There are two types of cameras in game development: perspective and orthographic. We are all familiar with how perspective works: the farther an object is from the camera or your eyes, the smaller it appears. This is great for 3D games, as a scene will be rendered realistically. However, perspective cameras are not as useful for 2D games, since there really is no need for perspective besides maybe zooming in and out, which is not something that you see very often. Instead, you will use an orthographic camera, which works exactly like the perspective camera, except that it does not care about how far objects are from it. Everything will be drawn with the same dimensions on the screen, whether objects are right in front of the camera or a thousand miles away.

As shown in Figure 3-2, objects are placed in the game using world coordinates and may have a different coordinate system, with a different origin and axis pointing in different directions than the MonoGame 2D rendering target. The job of the camera is to take world coordinates and transform them into screen coordinates and it accomplishes this using different transformations, namely translations, rotations, and scaling.

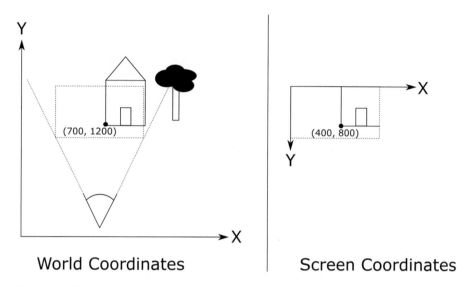

World Coordinates   **Screen Coordinates**

Figure 3-2. *Transforming world coordinates to screen coordinates*

In your game, however, you will keep things simple and use the same X and Y axis that MonoGame uses so no transformation will be needed. Also, since you are not using any perspective, you do not need to create what is called a projection, where objects closer to the camera that are projected to the screen look bigger than objects further away. However, you will also have a camera that is positioned directly in the middle of the viewport, dead center in the middle of your game screen. Your camera will be able to rotate and zoom as well, so you need to take that into account as you transform world objects into screen objects.

First, you need to deal with the fact that you have two different coordinate systems with two different origins: the world origin and the camera origin. To create the illusion that when the camera zooms in or out, or rotates, you need to transform your objects based on the camera's origin, not the world origin.

In MonoGame, when you want to rotate an object around its center point, you must first move the object's center point, or the object's origin, to the world's origin, perform the rotation, and move the object back to where it belongs. Otherwise, the object would rotate around the world's origin instead of its own origin and could very well fly out of the screen.

Similarly, to create the illusion that your camera is rotating, you need to bring the camera's origin to the world's origin, along with all the objects in the world, then rotate all the objects in the world, and finally move everything back. You proceed similarly to create the illusion that the camera is zooming in and out. The camera's origin must match the world's origin, and then you scale objects and move everything back. Thankfully, you can do the rotation and the scaling at the same time.

With the camera rotation and zoom taken care of, you just need to position the objects on the screen depending on where they are relative to the camera's origin. To do this, you simply need to move the world's origin to the camera's origin, translating all the world objects in the process.

So, for each game object, you want to

1. Move from the camera space to the world space using a translation from the camera's origin to the world's origin.

2. Scale and rotate the object.

3. Move the object back to where it was in the world by translating it by the inverse of the vector from step 1.

4. Move the object into the camera's coordinate system by translating it by a vector represented by the camera's position.

This is illustrated in Figure 3-3.

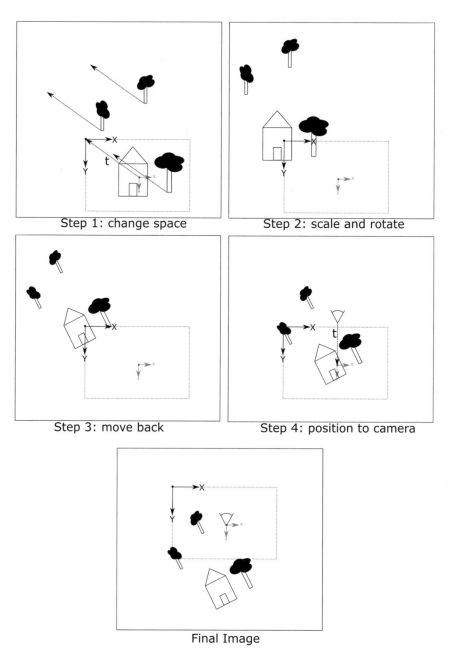

Figure 3-3. All the steps needed to generate an image with a camera

Adding a Camera to Your Game

Given the right knowledge of linear algebra and all the tutorials available on this subject on the Internet, it is not too hard to implement a camera system. MonoGame, however, already has libraries available that have good camera implementations. In this section, you will look at the MonoGame.Extended NuGet library and use the orthographic camera class that it offers.

First, open up the NuGet package manager for the solution (found in Tools ➤ NuGet Package Manager ➤ Manage NuGet Packages for Solutions), search for MonoGame.Extended, and select the package, as shown in Figure 3-4.

MonoGame.Extended by craftworkgames, 46.7K downloads   v3.8.0
It makes MonoGame more awesome.

Figure 3-4. *The MonoGame.Extended NuGet package*

Install the library for the Game project in the solution.

Next, let's create a new GameState for the game. The game you are improving uses a custom engine that loads instances of the GameState class to run the game. Each game state object owns its own input handler and game commands. This allows you to create test game states to experiment with the engine and try out new things. In this case, you create a new TestCameraState.cs file in the Game\States\Dev folder.

```
public class TestCameraState : BaseGameState
{
    private const string PlayerAnimationTurnLeft =
        "Sprites/Animations/FighterSpriteTurnLeft";
    private const string PlayerAnimationTurnRight =
        "Sprites/Animations/FighterSpriteTurnRight";
    private const string PlayerFighter =
        "Sprites/Animations/FighterSpriteSheet";
```

```
private PlayerSprite _playerSprite;
private OrthographicCamera _camera;

public override void LoadContent()
{
    var viewportAdapter = new DefaultViewportAdapter
    (_graphicsDevice);
    _camera = new OrthographicCamera(viewportAdapter);
    _playerSprite = new PlayerSprite(LoadTexture(Player
    Fighter),

                                LoadAnimation(Player
                                AnimationTurnLeft),
                                LoadAnimation(Player
                                AnimationTurnRight));
    _playerSprite.Position = new Vector2(0, 0);
}
}
```

The goal of this TestCameraState is to test the camera, so you need at least one game object to display on the screen and the PlayerSprite object is an ideal test subject. Initializing the PlayerSprite requires the two animation definitions we discussed in Chapter 2.

The class also has an OrthographicCamera from MonoGame.Extended, which is imported via these two import statements:

```
using MonoGame.Extended;
using MonoGame.Extended.ViewportAdapters;
```

The camera is instantiated in the LoadContent() method, called by the engine and MonoGame when it is time to load the assets necessary to run a specific game state class. The PlayerSprite is created the same way as in the GamePlayState class. The camera is instantiated by passing in a viewport adapter, but this is optional. Behind the scenes, MonoGame. Extended will create a default viewport adapter if one is not specified.

The viewport adapter is a simple wrapper around the concept of a viewport, which is basically what you see on the screen. It has a bounding rectangle, a height, and a width. The DefaultViewportAdapter looks at the supplied graphics device's viewport to set its internal width and height. In that sense, it is the same as the game's own viewport.

Then the orthographic camera is instantiated. Internally, MonoGame. Extended uses the following constructor:

```
public OrthographicCamera(ViewportAdapter viewportAdapter)
{
    _viewportAdapter = viewportAdapter;

    Rotation = 0;
    Zoom = 1;
    Origin = new Vector2(viewportAdapter.VirtualWidth/2f,
                         viewportAdapter.VirtualHeight/2f);
    Position = Vector2.Zero;
}
```

Your camera is created with a rotation angle of zero and a zoom value of 1. The interesting thing here, however, is that the camera has an origin that is set in the middle of the viewport. The camera's position, on the other hand, is set to **(0, 0)**. It's important to note that the two are independent of one another and are used in two different steps of converting world coordinates into screen coordinates. The camera's origin is in screen coordinates and is used to rotate and scale game objects around itself instead of the default MonoGame origin at (0, 0). The camera's position is its location in the game world, so it is in world coordinates. It is used to move game objects into the viewport or out of the viewport depending on where the camera is actually located in the world.

The Camera class offers some extra features you can use. It can move, be repositioned, zoom in or out, and rotate. It can also let you specify a minimum and maximum zoom level to prevent the user from going beyond set boundaries. It also has a bounding rectangle and some utility functions that let you query the camera to ask if it contains a Point, Vector, or Rectangle within its bounding rectangle. This will be useful to determine later if objects are visible on the screen. Finally, it also provides functions to convert screen coordinates to world coordinates and vice-versa. You will use the ScreenToWorld() functions in Chapter 4 when you create a level editor and need to determine the world coordinates of where your mouse just clicked.

You can now override the Render() method of the BaseStateClass:

```
public override void Render(SpriteBatch spriteBatch)
{
    var transformMatrix = _camera.GetViewMatrix();

    spriteBatch.Begin(transformMatrix: transformMatrix);
        _playerSprite.Render(spriteBatch);
    spriteBatch.End();
}
```

Your Render() method will only render the player sprite to the screen. The difference between that method and the base class is that you now provide the spriteBatch.Begin() method with a transform matrix that MonoGame will use to transform your game objects depending on where the camera is located in the game. That transform matrix is available by calling _camera.GetViewMatrix(). The indentation before the Render() line is an old habit of ours to easily visualize the code that is between the Begin() and End() calls and is purely esthetic.

Finally, the SetInputManager() and HandleInput() methods must be overridden to convert game commands into actionable events. The game state classes are expected to define input managers that know how to convert input captured from the mouse, keyboard, or gamepad, and transform them into predefined input commands, which are defined in DevInputCommand.cs. The input manager is given a mapper class,

defined in `DevInputMapper.cs`. The mapper and the commands cause
`HandleInput()` in the game state to receive a list of commands to handle,
like moving the camera around, moving the player, or quitting the game,
among others.

Making the Camera Travel Up with the Player

You will now recreate in your `TestCameraState` the part of the game where
the player is always moving up, but the camera needs to follow the player.
In the original game, the player does not really move. Instead, the game
objects move down to create the illusion that the player is flying up. Now,
however, you will make the player move up and the camera will follow
along for the ride.

First, move your attention to the player sprite object. In your new
paradigm, you want to have the player constantly move up into the game
world and the camera will follow at the same speed. The player game
object already has a default speed, so you can reuse that. Furthermore, you
want to retain the ability that the player has to move the fighter jet around
the screen. To do that, you need to increase the fighter jet speed when the
player presses the keyboard key that moves the player upwards. Then,
when the key is released, you will introduce a new behavior that causes the
player to slowly move back down towards the bottom of the screen. Finally,
when the player presses the key that moves the player downwards, the
player will accelerate towards the bottom of the screen.

The tactic to achieve this behavior is as follows: the player will move
slightly slower than the camera when no keys are being pressed. This will
cause the fighter sprite to move downwards since the camera moves up a
bit faster. But to prevent the player from being off screen, you need to
keep the sprite within the screen boundaries. To achieve that, the game
state will push the player up when it reaches the bottom of the screen.

Next, the player sprite will have a boost up speed and a boost down speed for when the up and down keys are pressed. Let's look at what changed for the PlayerSprite class:

```
private Vector2 _playerNormalUpSpeed = new Vector2(0, -8.0f);
private Vector2 _playerBoostUpSpeed = new Vector2(0, -15.0f);
private Vector2 _playerBoostDownSpeed = new Vector2(0, -6.0f);

public Vector2 CurrentUpSpeed { get; private set; }
```

Knowing that the camera speed will be **10.0**, you set the player's three different velocities to vectors that point upwards. The normal speed will be **8.0**, which is indeed a bit slower than the camera's 10.0 speed. But when boosted upward, the player will move up the screen at a speed of **15.0**, while only moving at a speed of **6.0** when being boosted backwards. You also have the CurrentUpSpeed property to allow the game state to set the player's speed based on keyboard input. When the player sprite is instantiated, it defaults to the _playerNormalUpSpeed velocity.

You also need a public method to reset the player's speed when no upward or downward keys are being pressed:

```
public void StopVerticalMoving()
{
    CurrentUpSpeed = _playerNormalUpSpeed;
}
```

Now you can change how the player moves. Instead of changing the object's position in the world when calling MoveUp() or MoveDown(), you change the player's current speed:

```
public void MoveUp()
{
    CurrentUpSpeed = _playerBoostUpSpeed;
}
```

```
public void MoveDown()
{
    CurrentUpSpeed = _playerBoostDownSpeed;
}
```

Finally, you change the player's position in the Update() method, simply by adding the current velocity vector to the current position:

```
public void Update(GameTime gametime)
{
    Position += CurrentUpSpeed;

    if (_currentAnimation != null)
    {
        _currentAnimation.Update(gametime);
    }
}
```

You can now move your attention back to the TestCameraState class. First, you set the default camera speed to 10.0:

```
private const float CAMERA_SPEED = 10.0f;
```

Then, during each Update() call, you update the PlayerSprite object and make the camera move up:

```
public override void UpdateGameState(GameTime gameTime)
{
    _playerSprite.Update(gameTime);
    _camera.Position += new Vector2(0, -CAMERA_SPEED);
}
```

Finally, to keep the player in bounds, you add a KeepPlayerInBounds() method that will be called at every update. The method verifies that the player sprite is within the camera's bounding rectangle by comparing each side of the player's bounds with each side of the camera's bounding rectangle and correcting the player's position to keep it in bounds. This is where the camera pushes the player upwards if it falls below the bottom edge of the screen.

```
private void KeepPlayerInBounds()
{
    if (_playerSprite.Position.X < _camera.BoundingRectangle.Left)
    {
        _playerSprite.Position = new Vector2(0, _playerSprite.
        Position.Y);
    }

    if (_playerSprite.Position.X + _playerSprite.Width >
        _camera.BoundingRectangle.Right)
    {
        _playerSprite.Position = new Vector2(
            _camera.BoundingRectangle.Right - _playerSprite.
            Width,
            _playerSprite.Position.Y);
    }

    if (_playerSprite.Position.Y < _camera.BoundingRectangle.Top)
    {
        _playerSprite.Position = new Vector2(
            _playerSprite.Position.X,
            _camera.BoundingRectangle.Top);
    }
```

```
if (_playerSprite.Position.Y + _playerSprite.Height >
    _camera.BoundingRectangle.Bottom )
{
    _playerSprite.Position = new Vector2(
        _playerSprite.Position.X,
        _camera.BoundingRectangle.Bottom - _playerSprite.
        Height);
}
}
```

Finally, you map the input commands to make the player move, making sure to call the KeepPlayerInBounds() method at the end. Note that the HandleInput() method is called by your engine during the Update phase of each frame.

```
public override void HandleInput(GameTime gameTime)
{
    InputManager.GetCommands(cmd =>
    {
        if (cmd is DevInputCommand.DevQuit)
        {
            NotifyEvent(new BaseGameStateEvent.GameQuit());
        }

        if (cmd is DevInputCommand.DevPlayerUp)
        {
            _playerSprite.MoveUp();
        }

        if (cmd is DevInputCommand.DevPlayerDown)
        {
            _playerSprite.MoveDown();
        }
```

```
if (cmd is DevInputCommand.DevPlayerRight)
{
    _playerSprite.MoveRight();
}

if (cmd is DevInputCommand.DevPlayerLeft)
{
    _playerSprite.MoveLeft();
}

if (cmd is DevInputCommand.DevPlayerStopsMoving
Horizontal)
{
    _playerSprite.StopMoving();
}

if (cmd is DevInputCommand.DevPlayerStopsMoving
Vertical)
{
    _playerSprite.StopVerticalMoving();
}

KeepPlayerInBounds();

    });
}
```

You can now invoke your new TestCameraState when the game starts to play with your new camera system. In Program.cs, replace the usage of the SplashState in the MainGame() constructor call with the TestCameraState:

```
using (var game = new MainGame(WIDTH, HEIGHT, new
TestCameraState(), DEBUG))
```

Now, running your game will run your test state and you can play around with the player sprite and the camera as they constantly move up in the game world.

Conclusion

In this chapter, we introduced the concept of a camera and explained how an orthographic camera works and how it can transform world coordinates into screen coordinates, opening up the possibility of manipulating a game world that is observed by a camera instead of manipulating objects on the screen. You then installed the MonoGame.Extended library and used its orthographic camera in your game, using a new game state class to avoid breaking the actual GamePlayState class.

CHAPTER 4

Level Editor

Let's switch your attention now to a building a level editor. The original game that you are working on upgrading used a very limited system to define its levels. It consisted of text files where each row of comma-separated fields described what was displayed on the screen. Those level files also did not contain any data for what to draw in the background since they assumed that there was an infinite scrolling background in the game.

As you saw in Chapter 3, you are moving away from a game platform that scrolls objects downwards. Instead, you are now using a camera that moves up through the world, which will force you to redefine how the game displays objects.

This seems like a good time to invest in building a proper level editor and looking at using new background tiles and objects to make the game prettier. OpenGameArt.org user Chabull has created a very nice set of tiles and objects for you to use here: `https://opengameart.org/users/chabull`.

It takes a lot of code to create a level editor and it will not be possible to cover everything, like how Windows Forms are created, how to bind events, the new level definition, and the pipeline extension to load and save levels. Most of this information is covered in other books and online tutorials, or other chapters of this book.

© Louis Salin and Rami Morrar 2022
L. Salin and R. Morrar, *Game Development with MonoGame*,
https://doi.org/10.1007/978-1-4842-7771-3_4

In this chapter, you will

- Learn how to embed a MonoGame display within a Window Forms application.

- Build a level editor to design, load, and save levels.

- Use an atlas to organize ground and building textures.

MonoGame.Forms

One of the challenges of building a level editor is being able to simultaneously have a game screen displaying the world as you are designing it and a user interface that presents all the textures available to use. The user interface should let you perform the following actions:

- Select a texture for use.

- Place a texture in the game world.

- Remove a texture from the game world.

- Save or load a level by pressing a button.

This mixing of game elements and UI elements is not trivial to achieve. A programmer could create a game state where the world is being displayed as if it was an actual game, but offer 2D UI elements like menus, lists, and buttons to click to give the player the ability to create, load, and save levels. This is a technique used in Nintendo's Mario Maker, for example, since all players are also level builders. It is also not very difficult to do if the programmer already has good 2D set of UI elements. In fact, you will build your own in a later chapter.

However, for those of us using Windows, the quickest way is to mix Windows Form elements with a game window displayed in the same application, as shown in Figure 4-1.

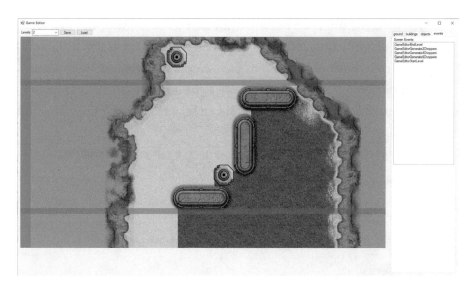

Figure 4-1. *Adding a MonoGame window to a Windows Forms application*

To achieve this, you will use MonoGame.Forms, a freely available library by Marcel Härtel that lets you treat a MonoGame window as a Windows Forms UI element that can be dragged and dropped into your level editor.

You can find the source code here: https://github.com/sqrMin1/ MonoGame.Forms. The documentation for the library can be found here: https://github.com/sqrMin1/MonoGame.Forms/blob/master/MonoGame. Forms.Readme.md.

How the Editor Works

Let's go over how to use the editor to create a level. As you can see in Figure 4-1, the biggest control on the screen is the GameControl from MonoGame.Forms. It is used to display the current level, which can be selected from the Levels drop-down selector at the top left of the screen. Switching between levels will cause the GameControl to start displaying the selected level.

When pressing the Load or Save buttons, the level editor will load or save the currently selected level. When loading a level, it will load an existing compiled .xnb level file. On the other hand, when saving a level, it will generate an .xml file that will need to be added to the asset pipeline and compiled into an .xnb file so that it can be used both by the game and the game editor.

Finally, on the right of the screen you have a tab control with four tabs:

- Ground

- Buildings

- Objects

- Events

Each tab contains a list of tiles, textures, game objects, or events that can be placed into the world. In addition, each tab represents a layer of the world to help you organize the drawing order of textures. Background tiles are drawn before buildings, which are drawn before game objects. We will detail this process further down.

Changing tabs in the tab control tells the game control which layer to use. Similarly, changing the currently selected item in the list views tells the game control which item to place into the world.

Creating the GameEditor Project

The MonoGame.Forms documentation is very good and getting a new project off the ground is straightforward, but you must first create a new Windows Application project in your solution that targets the .Net 4.8 Framework due to some compatibility issues. Right-click the solution and select Add and then New Project. Then, select the Windows Forms App (.NET Framework) template, as shown in Figure 4-2.

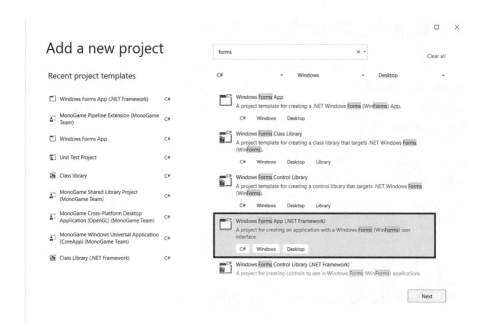

Figure 4-2. *Creating a new Windows Form project for your level editor*

Click Next and call the project **GameEditor**. You should now have a blank Windows Forms application to which will you add MonoGames.Form.

Installing MonoGame.Forms

Installing MonoGame.Forms can easily be done using NuGet. Right-click the project in the Solution Explorer and select Manage NuGet Packages. Then search for the MonoGame.Forms package and install MonoGame.Forms.DX, which is the DirectX version of the package. You could, alternatively, use the OpenGL version of the library, but it runs very slowly compared to the DirectX version. Even though your game uses OpenGL, you can build your level editor using DirectX if you know your level designers are Windows users. All in all, it does not make a big difference which one is chosen, besides the performance issues.

Creating the MonoGame Control

Now you need to create a Windows Form control that will host your MonoGame display. To do so, create a new class in the GameEditor project called GameControl and make it inherit MonoGame.Forms.Controls. MonoGameControl:

```
using Microsoft.Xna.Framework;
using MonoGame.Forms.Controls;

namespace GameEditor
{
    public class GameControl : MonoGameControl
    {
        protected override void Initialize()
        {
            base.Initialize();
        }

        protected override void Update(GameTime gameTime)
        {
            base.Update(gameTime);
        }

        protected override void Draw()
        {
            base.Draw();
        }
    }
}
```

This code overrides three basic MonoGame methods inherited from `MonoGameControl`: `Initialize()`, `Update()`, and `Draw()`. Those three methods are called by MonoGame whenever a scene needs to be initialized, updated, or drawn to the screen, just like in a regular game. Compile your code so Visual Studio can discover this new control.

You can now add the control to your form. First, rename `Form1.cs` to `GameEditorForm.cs` and allow Visual Studio to rename the classes as well. Then, double-click `GameEditorForm.cs` to see a blank Windows Form. In the Toolbox tab in Visual Studio, you should now see a `GameControl` that you can drag and drop onto your form, as seen in Figure 4-3.

Figure 4-3. *The toolbox showing your new GameControl*

Drag the control onto the form, as shown in Figure 4-4, and run your project. You should see a blue screen within your Windows application, as shown in Figure 4-5.

Figure 4-4. *Your Windows application with the MonoGame control, as seen from Visual Studio*

Figure 4-5. *Your blank MonoGame control in a running application*

You are now ready to start building your level editor!

Asset Management

In order to build your levels, you need to access your assets, which are built by the Content Pipeline Tool in the Game project. You could add a brand-new Content Pipeline Tool for the Game Editor, but that would entail duplicating your content pipeline and the required extensions needed to compile assets, and to make modifications twice in both the Game and the `GameEditor` whenever an asset is modified.

Instead, you will import the compiled `.xnb` asset files into the `GameEditor` in a directory structure that mimics the one found in the Game project. Thus, you will have fonts, levels, and sprites organized similarly to your current game assets.

Every time an asset is modified, it needs to be imported into the `GameEditor` project. This is not too hard to achieve by using Visual Studio's pre-build events.

The levels you create will be saved as `.xml` files. As shown in Figure 4-6, once saved, those level `.xml` files will need to be copied into your game assets and compiled there. But because you will use a content manager to load those levels, the `GameEditor` will need to have access to the compiled `.xnb` files to read the level data, which means you will need to copy the compiled level files back to the `GameEditor` content files and rebuild the project before being able to load each level.

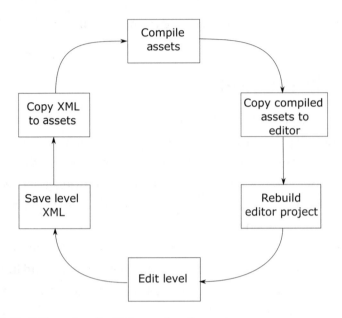

Figure 4-6. *Lifecycle of editing a level asset*

This is somewhat tedious but it can easily be automated using pre- and post-build events to copy the files.

Let's start by copying some `.xnb` files from your Game project into the game editor. First, create a new `Content` folder in the `GameEditor` directory. Then, create the following folders within the `Content` folder:

– `Sprites`

– `Levels`

– `Atlas`

You will eventually use all three folders, but let's first copy `Game\Content\bin\Windows\Sprites\ Turrets\Tower.xnb` into your `GameEditor\Content\Sprites` directory. The directory structure does not have to match exactly between the two projects, as long as you keep things organized.

From now on, working within a MonoGame forms control is very similar to working with MonoGame. For example, displaying the Tower sprite is as easy as loading it and rendering it within the control's Draw() method:

```
var tower = Editor.Content.Load<Texture2D>("Sprites\Tower");
Editor.spriteBatch.Draw(
    tower, new Rectangle(0, 0, tower.Width, tower.Height),
    Color.White);
```

The code looks familiar, with the difference that the Content Manager and the SpriteBatch are accessed via an Editor property that MonoGame. Forms controls.

Using a Better Set of Tiles and Game Objects

As discussed at the beginning of this chapter, you will update the game with a new set of background tiles and game objects. See Figures 4-8 and 4-9 for a snippet of what you will use.

Figure 4-7. *New background tiles to play with!*

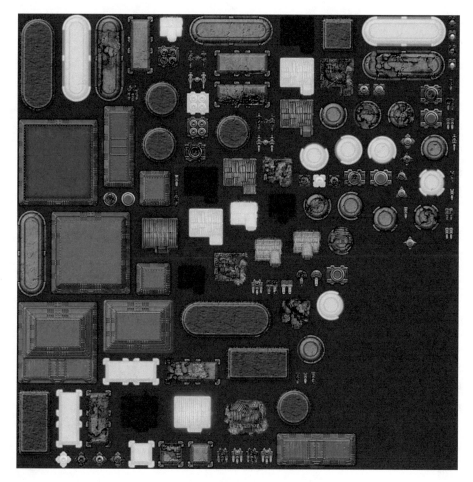

Figure 4-8. *New building textures to play with!*

The MonoGameControl Class

Let's take a very brief and quick look at what MonoGame.Forms offers us.
First, it is a UI control, which means it offers all the same events that a
regular Windows UI control does. For example, you can override the
OnMouseDown() method, which will get called whenever the user clicks
somewhere on the control itself. That will come in handy when you later

91

want to place objects into the world. You will also override `OnMouseDown()` and `OnMouseUp()`, both of which are methods that come from the `Control` base class.

The `MonoGameControl` class has everything needed to display a basic blue window on the screen and it inherits from a few base classes via an inheritance chain that goes as follow: `MonoGameControl` > `GameControl` > `GraphicsDeviceControl` > `Control`. Each one of these base classes has a specific responsibility and provides some utility methods you can use to build your level editor. It also gives you the important `Editor` property that allows you to access your favorite MonoGame objects, like the Content Manager and the `SpriteBatch`.

The `GameControl` base class gives your UI control the ability to tweak the game loop and only run a few frames at a time, or only update the world when the mouse is hovering over the control instead of the infinite 60 FPS that you are used to.

The `MonoGameControl` class also inherits from `GraphicsDeviceControl`, which manages access to the MonoGame graphic device. It also defines the `Initialize()` and `Draw()` abstract methods and offers you a few extra mouse-related events you can bind to.

Finally, the `GraphicsDeviceControl` base class sits directly on top of the `Control` class and is responsible for maintaining the graphics device.

Building Your Editor

Sitting down to build a level editor is a serious time investment and certain design elements must be considered before code is written.

First, is the level editor going to reuse existing scene rendering capabilities from the game or will it use its own? There are clear benefits from sharing code between the game and the level editor, since maintaining two graphical engines is a bit of overhead work. However, there are things you might want to do in the editor that are not allowed in the game. For example, you might want to zoom the camera out to fit a big level on the screen.

Another question is, how will you save the levels? What data schema will you use to store the level information? Are you reusing something that exists already or are you defining something completely new? In your case, you are redesigning the level structure and file format, so whatever you use for your level editor will be reused by the game. If the level editor can save and reload a level as a compiled asset, the game should have no trouble doing the same.

How are you going to place elements into your level? Your background tiles will fit nicely into a grid, but game objects like buildings and enemies could be anywhere, meaning you need to track their precise X and Y coordinates.

Finally, what UI controls are you going to use to allow the user to easily pick and choose tiles and objects to place in the level? In this case, you will auto-generate lists of tiles and objects that will be placed on different layers: background tiles will be on the background layer, buildings will be on the buildings layer, and game objects that you can interact with (and destroy) will be on the objects layer. Finally, you will have an event layer used to visualize a line on the level that when crossed by the user causes some kind of an event to be triggered, like generating choppers. Referring back to Figure 4-1, each layer is displayed on the right side of the screen in a tab control, where each tab represents the objects that can be placed on a single layer. Which layer should contain the selected object when it is placed down is set by which tab is currently selected in your MonoGame control.

These design decisions are completely objective and depend on the goals at hand. They are certainly not the most optimal way to build a level editor and will need to be revised over time as the game becomes more complex.

Setting the Stage

Given that you want to take a list of tiles and objects and place them in a world, you will need to implement the following features:

- Left-click to place a selected object.

- Right-click to remove the object under the mouse cursor from the currently selected layer.

- Middle-click and drag to move the camera around the world.

- Automatically populate the list of tiles and objects based on texture atlases.

- Select which level to edit.

- Load and save levels.

Adding a Camera

So right now your GameControl class displays a big blue square on the level editor. Let's change that. Let's color the area within the level with some kind of green color. Take a look at Figure 4-9, which shows a light blue and greener color inside the GameControl. If you are reading this in black and white, you should see two different shades of gray. The area depicted with the darker green color represents the area that will be displayed by the game as the camera scrolls up. The area in lighter blue represents an invisible area. This is useful to know where objects should be placed to be seen in the world.

When the level editor is started, it shows a clean slate. Everything is going to seem colored with the darker green color. But once the camera is put in place, you will be able to move it and expose the lighter blue areas of the world.

Figure 4-9. *Moving the camera exposes parts of the world that will be invisible in the game*

```
namespace GameEditor
{
    public class GameControl : MonoGameControl
    {
        private Texture2D _backgroundRectangle;
        private OrthographicCamera _camera;
        private bool _cameraDrag;

        protected override void Initialize()
        {
            base.Initialize();
```

```
            _backgroundRectangle = new Texture2D
            (GraphicsDevice, 1, 1);
            _backgroundRectangle.SetData(new[] { Color.
            CadetBlue });
            var viewportAdapter = new DefaultViewportAdapter
            (Editor.graphics);
            _camera = new OrthographicCamera(viewportAdapter);
            ResetCameraPosition();
            _draggedTile = null;

            OnInitialized(this, EventArgs.Empty);
        }
    }
}
```

This code declares three member variables: a background texture to draw the darker green color, the camera, and a Boolean flag that will be set to true whenever the middle mouse button is pressed, indicating that the camera will start moving around. Then, in the Initialize() method, you give each of those member variables a value and reset the camera position to the bottom of the game world:

```
private void ResetCameraPosition()
{
    _camera.Position = new Vector2(
        0,
        Level.LEVEL_LENGTH * TILE_SIZE - ClientSize.Height
    );
}
```

Here, TILE_SIZE is a constant set to 128 pixels wide, which is the exact width and height of each background tile seen in Figure 4-7. Level is a class that will be used by the level editor to hold level information while you are editing a level. You will examine it further down. Right now, however, you are only using the level length as a way to know how far down in the world you need to place the camera:

```
namespace GameEditor
{
    public class Level
    {
        public const int LEVEL_LENGTH = 100;
        public const int LEVEL_WIDTH = 10;
    }
}
```

That number, 100, is completely arbitrary and up to the designer. The width is the same as that in the previous game. Together, these two numbers indicate that the game world for each level is 10 tiles wide by 100 tiles high.

Now to drag the camera around the world, you will override the OnMouseMove(), OnMouseDown(), and OnMouseUp() methods that you are inheriting from your base classes:

```
private int _mouseX;
private int _mouseY;

protected override void OnMouseUp(MouseEventArgs e)
{
    base.OnMouseUp(e);

    if (e.Button == MouseButtons.Middle)
    {
        _cameraDrag = false;
    }
}
```

```
protected override void OnMouseMove(MouseEventArgs e)
{
    base.OnMouseMove(e);

    if (_cameraDrag)
    {
        _camera.Move(new Vector2(_mouseX - e.X, _mouseY - e.Y));
    }

    _mouseX = e.X;
    _mouseY = e.Y;
}

protected override void OnMouseDown(MouseEventArgs e)
{
    base.OnMouseDown(e);

    if (e.Button == MouseButtons.Middle)
    {
        _cameraDrag = true;
    }
}
```

Those three methods are called when the mouse interacts with the GameControl. The .NET Framework will call each one depending on which event was triggered. When you press down on the middle button, you set the _cameraDrag variable to true. Whenever you release the middle mouse button, the variable is reset to false. Finally, whenever you move the mouse, you check if the _cameraDrag variable is true. When this is the case, you move the camera in the opposite direction! This is important because moving the camera in the opposite direction will cause the world to move in same direction the mouse was moving, creating the illusion that you are dragging the world around with the mouse.

How much to move the camera depends on how far the mouse moved since the last time the OnMouseMove() method was called. You keep track of the last mouse position with the _mouseX and _mouseY member variables. To calculate how far to move the camera, you subtract the current mouse position from the previous mouse position and use the resulting vector in your call to _camera.Move().

Using an Atlas for Your Ground Tiles

Now that you can move your camera around, you need to load your background tiles and game textures into atlases. An atlas is simply a large texture that contains many smaller textures aggregated into a single image, kind of like a quilt made out of many different squares. Each part of an atlas is a texture with a position, a name, and coordinates about where it is located in the atlas.

You will use MonoGame.Extended's TextureAtlas class in your GameControl class:

```
public Dictionary<string, TextureAtlas> Atlas { get; private set; }

protected override void Initialize()
{
    Atlas = new Dictionary<string, TextureAtlas>();
    var groundTiles = GetGroundTiles();
    var buildingTiles = GetBuildingTiles();
    var objectTiles = GetGameObjects();
}
```

This part of the Initialize() method creates a dictionary object that will link layer names ("ground", "buildings" and "objects") to atlases containing all the textures needed for that layer. Let's take a look at GetGroundTiles():

```
private Dictionary<string, Rectangle> GetGroundTiles()
{
```

```
return new Dictionary<string, Rectangle>
{
    { "sand", new Rectangle(0, 0, 128, 128) },
    { "beach_tm_02_grass", new Rectangle(128, 0, 128, 128) },
    { "beach_tm_02", new Rectangle(256, 0, 128, 128) },
    { "beach_tm_01_grass", new Rectangle(384, 0, 128, 128) },
    { "beach_tm_01", new Rectangle(512, 0, 128, 128) },
    { "beach_tl_grass", new Rectangle(640, 0, 128, 128) },
    { "beach_tl", new Rectangle(768, 0, 128, 128) },
    { "beach_rm_05_grass", new Rectangle(896, 0, 128, 128)
},

    ...

}
}
```

The GetGroundTiles() method creates a dictionary that links texture names like "beach_tm_02_grass" to a Rectangle for that particular texture in the atlas. Writing this is a fairly laborious process and is currently hardcoded. It is not ideal and could be improved, just like you did for the animation data in a previous chapter, by instead saving it to an XML file and loading it via the Content Pipeline Tool.

You then create the ground texture atlas like this:

```
var groundAtlas = new TextureAtlas(GROUND, _groundTexture,
groundTiles);
```

MonoGame.Extended will take care of everything from now on. All you need to do on your end is add this atlas to your dictionary of atlases:

```
Atlas.Add(GROUND, groundAtlas);
```

You can now access your textures by name in the atlas like this:

```
var texture = Atlas[GROUND]["beach_tm_02_grass"];
```

Before you do all this, however, there is one thing you need to take care of, as usual. You need a way for the GameControl to tell the GameEditorForm that owns it when the control will be fully initialized. The problem is that the GameControl will own the list of textures for ground tiles and game objects, which the GameEditorForm will need to populate its list boxes. However, it cannot get access to them until the GameControl is fully initialized. You will add an event on the GameControl that will be triggered once it is initialized.

```
public event EventHandler<EventArgs> OnInitialized;
```

The OnInitialized() event is triggered at the bottom of the Initialize() method in the GameControl class, which will let your GameEditorForm know that it can finally access its list of textures.

In GameEditorForm, you listen for this event and start loading atlas texture names to the ground ListView that you have on your Windows Form, as shown in the following code:

```
public GameEditorForm()
{
    InitializeComponent();

    gameControl.ClientSize = new System.Drawing.Size(1280, 720);
    gameControl.OnInitialized += GameControl_OnInitialized;
}

private void GameControl_OnInitialized(object sender, System.
EventArgs e)
```

```
{
    foreach (var tile in gameControl.Atlas[GameControl.GROUND])
    {
        groundListView.Items.Add(tile.Name);
    }
}
```

Once your GameControl is initialized, the GameEditorForm receives the event and queries its list of GROUND atlas textures and adds the names to the ground ListView on the right side panel of the Game Editor.

The process then repeats for the building atlas and layer.

Adding, Moving, and Removing Objects from Levels

What you have done so far is load up giant texture images that contain many sub-images into three atlases (GROUND, BUILDINGS, and OBJECTS) that are referenced by the GameControl. Once initialized, your GameControl sends an event to the GameEditorForm to let it know that it can now query the names of all your individual textures in each atlas and display them in the UI, ready to be picked by the user so you can place them into the world. How you know which texture needs to be placed on which layer is a responsibility of the GameEditorForm, which monitors which tab is selected in the control on the right of the app, and which object or tile is selected within that tab. The following code handles this in the GameEditorForm.

First, you need to bind to selection events in the tab control and list view controls within the GameControl_OnInitialized() method:

```
private void GameControl_OnInitialized(object sender, System.
EventArgs e)
{
    InitializeListsOfTiles();

    groundListView.ItemSelectionChanged += GroundListView_
    ItemSelectionChanged;
    buildingsListView.ItemSelectionChanged += Buildings
    ListView_ItemSelectionChanged;
    objectsListView.ItemSelectionChanged += ObjectsListView_
    ItemSelectionChanged;
    listViewScreenEvents.ItemSelectionChanged +=
    ListViewScreenEvents_ItemSelectionChanged;

    objectTabControl.SelectedIndexChanged += ObjectTabControl_
    SelectedIndexChanged;
}
```

Once your list of tiles is initialized, as you have seen previously, you then go to each list view control located within each tab and bind to their ItemSelectionChanged event, which will tell you which item was just selected by the user. You also bind to the tab control's SelectedIndexChanged to know which tab was just selected.

Let's take a look at how the ground list view event handler is implemented:

```
private void GroundListView_ItemSelectionChanged(
    object sender, ListViewItemSelectionChangedEventArgs e)
{
    gameControl.CurrentElementName = e.Item.Text;
}
```

Nothing too complicated is done here. You simply set the game control's `CurrentElementName` property to the selected item's name, which is identical to one of the atlas' keys you initialized earlier.

The event handler that gets called when you change the selected tab is very similar:

```
private void ObjectTabControl_SelectedIndexChanged(object
sender, System.EventArgs e)
{
    gameControl.CurrentLayer = objectTabControl.SelectedTab.Text;
    gameControl.CurrentElementName = null;
}
```

You keep track of the current layer within the game control by remembering the name of the tab you are currently on. Then, you reset the current element name, because the previously selected item should not be allowed to be placed on a layer where it should not exist.

Now that you can keep track of the current selected layer and current selected item, you can add some code to place the item into the world based on where the mouse is clicking. Let's see how to do that in the `GameControl`'s `OnMouseDown()` method:

```
if (e.Button == MouseButtons.Left)
{
    if (CurrentElementName != null && CurrentElementName.Length > 0)
    {
        if (CurrentLayer == GROUND)
        {
            var point = GetGridCoordinates();

            if (point.X >= 0 && point.X < Level.LEVEL_WIDTH &&
                point.Y >= 0 && point.Y < Level.LEVEL_LENGTH)
```

```
        {
            GetGroundGrid()[point.X, point.Y] =
            CurrentElementName;
        }
    }
    else if (CurrentLayer == BUILDINGS)
    {
        var worldCoords = _camera.ScreenToWorld(_mouseX,
        _mouseY);
        GetBuildings().Add(new GameEditorTileData(Current
        ElementName, (int) worldCoords.X, (int)
        worldCoords.Y));
    }
    else if (CurrentLayer == OBJECTS)
    {
        var worldCoords = _camera.ScreenToWorld
        (_mouseX, _mouseY);
        GetObjects().Add(new GameEditorTileData
        (CurrentElementName, (int) worldCoords.X, (int)
        worldCoords.Y));
    }
    }
}
```

In this code, when the left mouse button is clicked in the world, you verify that you have a CurrentElementName. If you do not, that means the user has not selected an item and there is nothing to place down. Otherwise, you check which layer you should be on, depending on which tab in the UI is selected. If it is the "ground" tab, you place the tile down into a grid, since all the textures are the same size. If the current layer is "building" or "objects," then you first transform the mouse coordinates to world coordinates using the handy camera functions from MonoGame. Extended and add the building or object to its proper layer.

The GetGridCoordinates() function, shown below, converts mouse coordinates into world coordinates and then converts them into array indices that point to the tile you clicked in your 10x100 background 2D array.

```
private Point GetGridCoordinates()
{
    var worldCoords = _camera.ScreenToWorld(_mouseX, _mouseY);
    var gridX = (int) worldCoords.X / TILE_SIZE;
    var gridY = (int) worldCoords.Y / TILE_SIZE;

    return new Point(gridX, gridY);
}
```

Back in the previous function, the GetObjects(), GetBuildings(), and GetGroundGrid() functions are defined this way and expose the underlying data structure used to keep track of these objects:

```
private string[,] GetGroundGrid()
{
    return GetCurrentLevel().GroundGrid;
}

private List<GameEditorTileData> GetBuildings()
{
    return GetCurrentLevel().Buildings;
}

private List<GameEditorTileData> GetObjects()
{
    return GetCurrentLevel().Objects;
}
```

GetCurrentLevel() returns an instance of the Level class in the project, which is responsible for holding all the data that will need to be saved to your level .xml file. Since the UI currently offers the choice of editing five different levels, GetCurrentLevel() will pick the currently selected level and then return the ground tiles, list of buildings, or the list of objects. You can see here that the ground grid is a simple two-dimensional array, while the buildings and objects are lists of GameEditorTileData, which is defined this way:

```
public class GameEditorTileData
{
    public string Name { get; set; }
    public int X { get; set; }
    public int Y { get; set; }

    public GameEditorTileData() { }

    public GameEditorTileData(string name, int x, int y)
    {
        Name = name;
        X = x;
        Y = y;
    }
}
```

Above, each tile or object has a name and a position in the world. This information will be saved when you hit the Save button.

To remove objects, you wait until the right mouse button is clicked and iterate through all objects of the current layer until you find one for whom the mouse coordinates fall within its bounding box. If found, you remove the object from the layer. In the OnMouseDown() method, you add this:

```
if (e.Button == MouseButtons.Right)
{
    if (CurrentLayer == GROUND)
    {
        var point = GetGridCoordinates();
        GetGroundGrid()[point.X, point.Y] = null;
    }
    else if (CurrentLayer == BUILDINGS)
    {
        var tile = GetAtlasTileFromCoords(BUILDINGS,
        GetBuildings());
        GetBuildings().Remove(tile);
    }
    else if (CurrentLayer == OBJECTS)
    {
        var tile = GetObjectTileFromCoords();
        GetObjects().Remove(tile);
    }
}
```

The code here makes sure you click the right mouse button. Then, if the current layer is the ground layer, you get the grid coordinate that matches the mouse coordinates and set that grid tile to null. Otherwise, if the current layer is either the buildings or objects layer, you try to find a building or object located under the mouse cursor, as shown in the following code, and remove it from the layer.

```
private GameEditorTileData GetAtlasTileFromCoords(
    string atlasName, List<GameEditorTileData> tileList)
{
    var worldCoords = _camera.ScreenToWorld(_mouseX, _mouseY);

    // find which object was clicked on
    foreach (var tile in tileList)
```

```
    {
        var tileLocationInWorld = new Rectangle(
            tile.X, tile.Y,
            Atlas[atlasName][tile.Name].Bounds.Width,
            Atlas[atlasName][tile.Name].Bounds.Height);

        if (tileLocationInWorld.Contains(worldCoords))
        {
            return tile;
        }
    }

    return null;
}
```

Once again, you convert mouse coordinates to world coordinates and iterate through all the objects within a list until you find one which has a bounding box that contains the point.

Now that your items are in memory inside a Level object, it is time to draw them.

Drawing Items on the Screen

Drawing your textures should be familiar. During the Draw() method call, you iterate through all the ground items first to display them. Then, you iterate through your buildings so they get drawn on top of the ground, followed by objects on top of buildings.

```
protected override void Draw()
{
    base.Draw();

    var transformMatrix = _camera.GetViewMatrix();
```

```
    Editor.spriteBatch.Begin(transformMatrix: transformMatrix);
    Editor.spriteBatch.Draw(
        _backgroundRectangle,
        new Rectangle(-5, -5, TILE_SIZE * Level.LEVEL_WIDTH + 10,
                      TILE_SIZE * Level.LEVEL_LENGTH + 10),
        Color.White);

    DrawGround();
    DrawBuildings();
    DrawObjects();
    Editor.spriteBatch.End();
}

private void DrawGround()
{
    for (int y = 0; y < Level.LEVEL_LENGTH; y++)
    {
        for (int x = 0; x < Level.LEVEL_WIDTH; x++)
        {
            DrawGridElement(GROUND, GetCurrentLevel().
            GroundGrid[x, y], x, y);
        }
    }
}

private void DrawBuildings()
{
    foreach (var obj in GetBuildings())
    {
        DrawAtlasTile(_buildingTexture, BUILDINGS, obj.Name,
        obj.X, obj.Y);
    }
}
```

```
private void DrawObjects()
{
    foreach (var obj in GetObjects())
    {
        var gameObject = GameObjects[obj.Name];
        var rectangle = new Rectangle(
            obj.X,
            obj.Y,
            gameObject.Width,
            gameObject.Height
        );

        Editor.spriteBatch.Draw(
            gameObject.Texture, rectangle, gameObject.Texture.
            Bounds,
            Color.White);
    }
}

private void DrawAtlasTile(
    Texture2D texture, string atlasName,
    string tileName, int x, int y)
{
    if (tileName != null && tileName != "")
    {
        var rectangle = new Rectangle(
            x,
            y,
            Atlas[atlasName][tileName].Width,
            Atlas[atlasName][tileName].Height
        );
```

```
        Editor.spriteBatch.Draw(
            texture, rectangle,
            Atlas[atlasName][tileName].Bounds, Color.White);
    }
}

private void DrawGridElement(string atlasName, string tileName,
int x, int y)
{
    if (tileName != null && tileName != "")
    {
        var rectangle = new Rectangle(
            x * TILE_SIZE,
            y * TILE_SIZE,
            TILE_SIZE,
            TILE_SIZE
        );
        Editor.spriteBatch.Draw(
            _groundTexture, rectangle,
            Atlas[atlasName][tileName].Bounds, Color.White);
    }
}
```

There is not much to discuss in this code. Most of the logic here iterates over objects to draw, decides where to draw them on the screen, and uses the Editor.spriteBatch() function to draw them.

Adding Game Events

Game events are the last type of "object" you can place into the world. These events are triggered when the player crosses a horizontal line in the world, which will happen at some point since the player is forced upwards constantly.

When crossed, the event triggers and the game will perform some action, like displaying text that the level is starting, congratulating the player for ending the level, or generating enemy choppers. The list of possible events is described in the **PipelineExtensions** project, since you will want to save them with the level data:

```
namespace PipelineExtensions
{
    public class GameEditorEvent
    {
        public int Y { get; set; }

        public static GameEditorEvent GetEvent(string typeName)
        {
            var fullyQualifiedName = $"PipelineExtensions.
            {typeName}";
            var eventType = Type.GetType(fullyQualifiedName);

            if (eventType != null)
            {
                return (GameEditorEvent) Activator.Create
                Instance(eventType);
            }

            return null;
        }
    }
}
```

```
public class GameEditorGenerate2Choppers : GameEditorEvent
{
    public GameEditorGenerate2Choppers() { }
}

public class GameEditorGenerate4Choppers : GameEditorEvent
{
    public GameEditorGenerate4Choppers() { }
}

public class GameEditorGenerate6Choppers : GameEditorEvent
{
    public GameEditorGenerate6Choppers() { }
}

public class GameEditorStartLevel : GameEditorEvent
{
    public GameEditorStartLevel() { }
}

public class GameEditorEndLevel : GameEditorEvent
{
    public GameEditorEndLevel() { }
}
}
```

Each event has a Y coordinate indicating the trigger line. They also have a utility method that allows the code to instantiate an event based on a string with the name of the event type. This will be useful when loading levels, since the event name will be a string inside the .xml file, or when you display the event types inside the tab control to allow the user to pick an event to display. The GetEvent() function above takes a string as a parameter and tries to create a new instance of an Event object that matches the event name.

Events have their own layer in the GameControl and are displayed as thin, semi-transparent, red rectangles on the screen. You might recall noticing them in Figure 4-1 at the beginning of this chapter.

They can be added and removed from the screen with left and right mouse button clicks, just like objects and buildings.

The list of available events is manually added to the list view shown in Figure 4-10 using the following code in the GameEditorForm class:

```
listViewScreenEvents.Items.Add(typeof(GameEditorGenerate2
Choppers).Name);
listViewScreenEvents.Items.Add(typeof(GameEditorGenerate4
Choppers).Name);
listViewScreenEvents.Items.Add(typeof(GameEditorGenerate6
Choppers).Name);
listViewScreenEvents.Items.Add(typeof(GameEditorStartLevel).Name);
listViewScreenEvents.Items.Add(typeof(GameEditorEndLevel).Name);
```

Figure 4-10. List of available events

When the user selects an event and clicks in the level, you find the class name that matches the name and add it to your list of events for the current level.

We will not cover the code that manages events on the GameControl screen since it is very similar to what we covered already, but let's take a quick peek at an extra feature added just for events in the game editor. Since all events look the same on the game screen, you need a way to identify them. When you hover the mouse cursor over them, you will display event details in the bottom left corner of the application, as show in Figure 4-11.

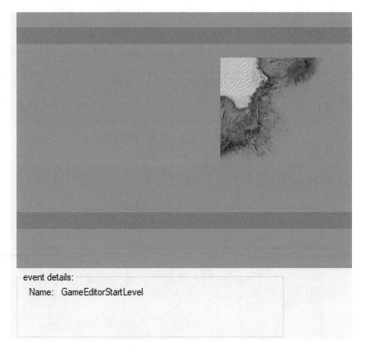

Figure 4-11. Event details shown on the screen

To achieve this, you monitor the mouse movement and as soon as the mouse hovers over one of those red rectangles, you trigger a .NET event that the GameEditorForm will listen to and display the game event details.

Looking at the OnMouseMove() method, you add

```
var evt = GetEventFromCoords();
if (evt != null)
{
    OnEventSelected(this, new EventSelectedArgs(this, evt));
}
else
{
    OnEventDeselected(this, EventArgs.Empty);
}
```

The two events are defined like this:

```
public event EventHandler<EventSelectedArgs> OnEventSelected;
public event EventHandler<EventArgs> OnEventDeselected;
```

Then, the GameEditorForm binds to those events like this:

```
gameControl.OnEventSelected += GameControl_OnEventSelected;
gameControl.OnEventDeselected += GameControl_OnEventDeselected;
```

with the event handlers coded as follows:

```
private void GameControl_OnEventSelected(object sender,
EventSelectedArgs e)
{
    groupBoxEventDetails.Visible = true;
    labelEventDetails.Text = e.GameEditorEvent.GetType().Name;
}
```

117

```
private void GameControl_OnEventDeselected(object sender,
System.EventArgs e)
{
    groupBoxEventDetails.Visible = false;
}
```

Conclusion

In this chapter, you learned the essentials of creating a level editor, with the ultimate goal of being able to generate levels that can be loaded later by the game and displayed exactly in the same way the level editor displays them, with the small difference that the game will not really show game events on the screen.

We did not look at all the code that was written, unfortunately, because that would have taken quite a bit of time. We did not fully explore the data structure used to store level data because it is a simple holder of arrays and lists. And although the Level object contains the methods needed to save and load levels, we already covered how to do this in the chapter on pipeline extensions.

With this knowledge in mind, you should be able to take the other texture atlases offered by Chabull on the Open Game Art website (see the link at the beginning of the chapter) and add them to the editor!

CHAPTER 5

Scripting

What Is Scripting?

As we all know, game logic doesn't write itself. All games use programming languages of some kind to make the game work. Most game engines and frameworks use a variety of languages, such as Python, Java, and C++. In MonoGame's case, C# is the language used to script gameplay behavior and functionality. C# is a versatile language that is compatible with multiple .NET libraries and has an easy syntax to understand, making it a go-to language for simple programming with a lot of freedom at your disposal to write your own logic.

In this section, you will be making a game from scratch. You'll be using a set of tools to animate, move, and add gravity/interactions to a player object, plus sound effects. You will also explore third-party libraries and software to expand your options and make your development process much easier.

© Louis Salin and Rami Morrar 2022
L. Salin and R. Morrar, *Game Development with MonoGame*,
https://doi.org/10.1007/978-1-4842-7771-3_5

Sprite Animation and Sound

A game would be very boring if all you had were just blocks as characters and single color backgrounds with no sound. Game worlds are usually filled with charming characters with vibrant colors and colorful worlds with wonderful vibrations in them.

You will be making a small little platformer game that includes the following throughout this book:

- Player control

- Camera script

- UI and menus

- Scripting (collision detection, player interaction)

- Enemy A.I.

- A boss battle

You're going to be making your own sprite animation player, as well as using an `InputManager` made by fellow GitHub user Thom Bakker (https://github.com/A1rPun/MonoGame.InputManager)

You will also be using the `Rectangle` struct that comes with MonoGame and will be making your own `Circle` struct to handle collisions, as well as the `SoundEffects` and `Song` classes to handle audio, and the `SpriteEffects` class as a helper with your sprite animation.

Note   Not all sprite sheets will have the same width and height ratio for all animations to be fitted for the `SpriteAnimation` class. If there is a lot of variation in sprites, we recommend cutting multiple sprites into comic strips for your project and keeping the width and height of each strip the same size if possible for smoother animation.

Load in your content within the Pipeline Tool as shown in Figure 5-1.

Figure 5-1. *All your content in the MonoGame Pipeline Tool*

You will then use your own SpriteAnimation class, as seen here:

```
public class SpriteManager
    {
        protected Texture2D Texture;
        public Vector2 Position = Vector2.Zero;
        public Color Color = Color.White;
        public Vector2 Origin;
        public float Rotation = 0f;
public float Scale = 1f;
        public SpriteEffects SpriteEffect;
        protected Rectangle[] Rectangles;
        protected int FrameIndex = 0;

        public SpriteManager(Texture2D Texture, int frames)
        {
            this.Texture = Texture;
            int width = Texture.Width / frames;
            Rectangles = new Rectangle[frames];

            for (int i = 0; i < frames; i++)
                Rectangles[i] = new Rectangle(i * width, 0,
                width, Texture.Height);
        }

        public void Draw(SpriteBatch spriteBatch, SpriteEffects
        effect)
        {
        spriteBatch.Draw(Texture,
                    Position,
                    Rectangles[FrameIndex],
                    Color,
                    Rotation,
```

```
                    Origin,
                    Scale,
                    effect,
                    0f);
    }
}

public class SpriteAnimation : SpriteManager
{
    private float timeElapsed;
    public bool IsLooping = true;
    private float timeToUpdate;
    public int FramesPerSecond { set { timeToUpdate = (1f
    / value); } }

    public SpriteAnimation(Texture2D Texture,
                           int frames,
                           int fps) : base(Texture, frames)
    {
        FramesPerSecond = fps;
    }

    public void Update(GameTime gameTime)
    {
  timeElapsed += (float)gameTime.ElapsedGameTime.
  TotalSeconds;
        if (timeElapsed > timeToUpdate)
        {
            timeElapsed -= timeToUpdate;
            if (FrameIndex < Rectangles.Length - 1)
                FrameIndex++;
            else if (IsLooping)
                FrameIndex = 0;
```

```
            }
        }
        public void setFrame(int frame)
        {
            FrameIndex = frame;
        }
    }
```

What this class is doing is splitting up your images one by one like a comic strip. Then it cycles through each slice of that image to render it in game time, as demonstrated in Figure 5-2.

Figure 5-2. *Spliting each image*

Figure 5-2 is a strip of sprites that will be divided into three separate instances with your SpriteAnimation class. Each frame of animation is divided by the image's width.

In the solution provided, you load all the player's animations in the LoadContent() method in your Game root class. Your player class has five animations in total, so let's put them into an array so you can switch between each one using some simple logic.

Here are the variables you'll be using to manipulate the player class:

```
/// <summary>
///  Player Sprites and Animation Field
/// </summary>
int AnimState;
private Texture2D idle, Jump, run, Damaged, punch, Fist;
public SpriteAnimation anim;
public SpriteAnimation[] animations = new SpriteAnimation[5];
```

Next, you will actually load in and initialize your animations and set the default animation to "idle."

```
idle = Content.Load<Texture2D>("Characters/Player/
PlayerIdle");
run = Content.Load<Texture2D>("Characters/Player/
PlayerRun");
punch = Content.Load<Texture2D>("Characters/Player/
PlayerPunch");
Fist = Content.Load<Texture2D>("Characters/Player/
PlayerFist");
Jump = Content.Load<Texture2D>("Characters/Player/
PlayerJump");
Damaged = Content.Load<Texture2D>("Characters/Player/
PlayerDamaged");
            animations[0] = new SpriteAnimation(idle, 4, 8);
            animations[1] = new SpriteAnimation(run, 3, 8);
            animations[2] = new SpriteAnimation(Jump, 2, 1);
            animations[3] = new SpriteAnimation(punch, 4, 8);
            animations[4] = new SpriteAnimation(Damaged, 1, 1);
// Sets the default animation to Idle
            player.anim = animations[0];
```

Currently in this GameRoot scene you have a player character that is moving around. You also have added some basic collision with the terrain and animation states, and you drew a sprite effects Flip method in order to flip the sprite. If you play it right now, you will have a player character being affected by gravity who is able to move left, right, jump, punch, and collide with the terrain.

```
using Microsoft.Xna.Framework;
using Microsoft.Xna.Framework.Graphics;
using Microsoft.Xna.Framework.Input;
```

125

```
using Chapter6Game.Content;
using System.Diagnostics;
using MonoGame.Extended;
using Chapter6Game.Content.Objects;
using MonoGame.Extended.ViewportAdapters;

 public class GameRoot: Game
{
 OrthographicCamera camera;

        InputManager Input;
        public Vector2 CameraPos;
        Player player = new Player();
        Terrain terrain = new Terrain();

        public Rectangle[] groundRectangles;
        bool flip = false;

        private GraphicsDeviceManager _graphics;
        private SpriteBatch _spriteBatch;

        private Texture2D background { get; set; }
        /// <summary>
        ///  Player Sprites and Animation Field
        /// </summary>
        int AnimState;
        private Texture2D idle, Jump, run, Damaged, punch, Fist;
        public SpriteAnimation anim;
        public SpriteAnimation[] animations = new
        SpriteAnimation[5];
        public Effect effect;
        public GameRoot()
        {
            Input = new InputManager(this);
```

```csharp
            _graphics = new GraphicsDeviceManager(this);
            Content.RootDirectory = "Content";
            IsMouseVisible = true;
        }
        protected override void Initialize()
        {
    this.Components.Add(Input);
var viewportAdapter = new BoxingViewportAdapter(Window,
GraphicsDevice, 360, 360);
            camera = new OrthographicCamera(viewportAdapter);
            _graphics.PreferredBackBufferWidth = 800;
            _graphics.PreferredBackBufferHeight = 800;
            _graphics.ApplyChanges();
            player.Initialize();
            terrain.Initialize();
            CameraPos = player.position -= new Vector2(-35, 50);
            base.Initialize();
        }

        protected override void LoadContent()
        {
    _spriteBatch = new SpriteBatch(GraphicsDevice);
idle = Content.Load<Texture2D>("Characters/Player/PlayerIdle");
run = Content.Load<Texture2D>("Characters/Player/PlayerRun");
punch = Content.Load<Texture2D>("Characters/Player/
PlayerPunch");
Fist = Content.Load<Texture2D>("Characters/Player/PlayerFist");
Jump = Content.Load<Texture2D>("Characters/Player/PlayerJump");
Damaged = Content.Load<Texture2D>("Characters/Player/
PlayerDamaged");
            animations[0] = new SpriteAnimation(idle, 4, 8);
            animations[1] = new SpriteAnimation(run, 3, 8);
```

```
            animations[2] = new SpriteAnimation(Jump, 2, 1);
            animations[3] = new SpriteAnimation(punch, 4, 8);
            animations[4] = new SpriteAnimation(Damaged, 1, 1);
            // Sets the default animation to Idle
            player.anim = animations[0];
            background = Content.Load<Texture2D>("Terrain/Sky");
            terrain.LoadContent(Content);
            effect = Content.Load<Effect>("PixelShader");
        }

protected override void Update(GameTime gameTime)
        {
        if (GamePad.GetState(PlayerIndex.One).Buttons.
        Back == ButtonState.Pressed || Keyboard.GetState().
        IsKeyDown(Keys.Escape))
            Exit();
            Input.Update(gameTime);
            camera.LookAt(CameraPos);
            if (Input.IsPressed(Keys.W) && !player.hasjumped)
            {
                player.anim = animations[2];
                Debug.WriteLine(AnimState);
                player.position.Y -= 10;
                player.gravity = - 5f;
                player.hasjumped = true;
            }
            else
            {
                AnimState = 0;
            }

            if (Input.IsPressed(Keys.K))
```

```
{
    AnimState = 3;
}
else
{
    AnimState = 0;
    player.anim = animations[0];
}

if (Input.IsPressed(Keys.A) !player.isCollidingside )
{
        flip = true;
        AnimState = 1;
        player.position.X -= player.speed;
        CameraPos.X -= player.speed;
}
else
{
    player.anim = animations[0];
}
if (Input.IsPressed(Keys.D) !player.isCollidingside)
{
flip = false;
CameraPos.X += player.speed;
player.position.X = player.position.X +    player.speed;
AnimState = 1;
}
AnimStates();
player.Update(gameTime);
base.Update(gameTime);
}
```

```
public  void AnimStates()
{
    switch (AnimState)
    {
        case 1:
        AnimState = 1;
      player.anim = animations[1];
        break;
        case 2:
            AnimState = 2;
            player.anim = animations[2];
            break;
        case 3:
            AnimState = 3;
            player.anim = animations[3];
            break;
    }
}

protected override void Draw(GameTime gameTime)
    {
GraphicsDevice.Clear(Color.CornflowerBlue);
var transFormMatrix = camera.GetViewMatrix();
_spriteBatch.Begin(SpriteSortMode.Immediate, BlendState.
AlphaBlend, transformMatrix: transFormMatrix);
effect.CurrentTechnique.Passes[0].Apply();
_spriteBatch.Draw(background, new Vector2(-471, 50), Color.White);
_spriteBatch.Draw(background, new Vector2(0, 50), Color.White);
_spriteBatch.Draw(background, new Vector2(471, 50), Color.White);
                if (flip)
                {
```

```
        player.anim.Draw(_spriteBatch, SpriteEffects.Flip
    Horizontally);
                }
                else
                {
player.anim.Draw(_spriteBatch, SpriteEffects.None);
                }
            terrain.Draw(_spriteBatch);
             _spriteBatch.End();
              base.Draw(gameTime);
        }
    }
}
```

Figure 5-3. *A simple texture shader implemented in the game*

As you can see in Figure 5-3, the player character sprite and the tiles/
background look very different from what is seen in the content pipeline.
This is because you are using what is called a shader.

What Is a Shader?

A shader is a program that is processed by the graphics processing unit (GPU) that manipulates the GPU into rendering certain graphical effects in your program. For this project, you're adding a very simple color palette change to every object on the scene to give it a little retro effect. If you comment out this code in the Draw() method of the game root

```
effect.CurrentTechnique.Passes[0].Apply();
```

the game will render the sprites' original colors.

You do this by loading an Effect class into your pipeline. This is what is inside the PixelShader.fx file.

```
#if OPENGL
    #define SV_POSITION POSITION
    #define VS_SHADERMODEL vs_3_0
    #define PS_SHADERMODEL ps_3_0
#else
    #define VS_SHADERMODEL vs_4_0_level_9_1
    #define PS_SHADERMODEL ps_4_0_level_9_1
#endif

Texture2D SpriteTexture;

sampler s0;
sampler2D SpriteTextureSampler = sampler_state
{
    Texture = <SpriteTexture>;
};
struct VertexShaderOutput
{
    float4 Position : SV_POSITION;
    float4 Color : COLOR0;
```

```
    float2 TextureCoordinates : TEXCOORD0;
};

float4 MainPS(VertexShaderOutput input) : COLOR0
{
    float4 color = tex2D(s0, input.TextureCoordinates);
    color.r = color.r * 255;
    color.g = color.g ;
    color.b = color.b  /2;
    return color;
}
technique SpriteDrawing
{
    pass P0
    {
        PixelShader = compile PS_SHADERMODEL MainPS();
    }
};
```

MonoGame uses High-Level Shading Language (HLSL) to render shaders onto your scene. You can create one by going to your Content Pipeline Tool, creating a new item, and then clicking **Effect**.

What you really want to look at here is the float4 MainPS(VertexShaderOutput input) method within HLSL. You take in a float4 to represent your colors and pass it in through a tex2D struct, which affects all your Texture2Ds within MonoGame. The color variables represent the colors of red (color.r), green (color.g), and blue (color.b) on a computer. You can manipulate these values from a scale of 0-255 (the range of RGB colors) to give you a nice looking shader for your sprites. We recommend playing around with these values and finding something nice that will fit your game. Do note that although shaders use the same .fx file as particles, they are handled completely differently (more on particles later).

And since shaders are rendered before the GPU processes them, you can't manipulate them when they're already rendered on the screen.

Now let's talk about some more practical applications like pausing the game and putting collectibles like coins in your game.

Pausing the Game

Pausing the game is simple. You put in all the objects that are being updated per frame, such as your player character, enemies, projectiles, and collectibles, into a single pause Boolean and wrap a pause Boolean around them like so in your Update() method:

```
bool paused = false;
 if (!paused)
          {
          camera.LookAt(CameraPos);
          }
          Input.Update(gameTime);
          if (Input.IsPressed(Keys.P))
          {
              paused = true;
          } else if (Input.IsPressed(Keys.O))
          {
              paused = false;
          }
 if (!paused)
          {
              AnimStates();
              player.Update(gameTime);
          }
```

You will need to go back later to enemies and collectibles to be put in your pause function. Putting them under the pause boolean stops them from moving in the scene. For now let's focus on using scripting a new collision struct to collect coins for your game.

Circle Struct

As you can see in the `Player` and `Terrain` classes, you are using a `Rectangle` struct in order to detect collisions and do collision interaction with the player. This is ok for objects that can fit into a more rectangular shape, but for more circular items it can become a bit weird to get the collision right. It's also not very efficient for optimizing your game to use less memory. You can remedy this by creating your own `Circle` struct.

Your `Circle` struct is simple. You take the radius of your circle defined as a float and calculate the distance between the sides of each rectangle. If your distance is less than the sum of the radius of the circle and sides of the rectangle, you have found a collision.

In the `Circle.cs` file, you can see that with the help of the `MathHelper` class found in the MonoGame framework this calculation becomes very simple:

```
using Microsoft.Xna.Framework;
namespace Chapter6Game.Content
{   public struct Circle
    {
        public Vector2 Center;
        public float Radius;
        // Constructor to be used for your Circle
        public Circle(Vector2 Position, float radius)
        {
            Center = Position;
            Radius = radius;
```

```
        }
        public bool Intersects(Rectangle rectangle)
        {
    Vector2 v = new Vector2(MathHelper.Clamp(Center.X,
    rectangle.Left, rectangle.Right),
MathHelper.Clamp(Center.Y, rectangle.Top, rectangle.Bottom));

            Vector2 direction = Center - v;
            float distanceSquared = direction.LengthSquared();

            return ((distanceSquared >= 0) && (distanceSquared
            < Radius * Radius));
        }
    }
}
```

In the Coins.cs file where your Coins class is, you can see this being
used in its Update method:

```
using Chapter6Game.Content.Objects;
using Microsoft.Xna.Framework;
using Chapter6Game;
using Chapter6Game.Content;
using System.Diagnostics;

namespace MiniMan.Content.Objects
{
  public class Coins
    {
        Player player = new Player();
        public Vector2 Position;
        public Rectangle coinRect;
        public SpriteAnimation anim;
```

```csharp
        public Coins(GameRoot root)
        {
            Position = new Vector2(-600, 390);
            player = root.player;

          // coinRect  = new Rectangle((int)Position.X, (int)
          Position.Y, 32, 32);
        }
        public void Update (GameTime gameTime)
        {
            anim.Update(gameTime);
            anim.Position = Position;

            HandleCollision();
        }
        public Circle BoundingCircle
        {
            get
            {
                return new Circle(Position,  10 );
            }
        }

    public void HandleCollision()
        {
            if (BoundingCircle.Intersects(player.playerRect))
            {

                Debug.WriteLine("Circle Collision Found");
            }
        }
    }
}
```

If you run the program, you can see that the collision works and your circle collision is being detected in the console window.

Now you must set something else up that is equally as important. And this is a simple UI to display your health.

Displaying Health

You want to be able to have the player display their health so that whenever the player gets hit, it can be shown through three hearts. Here is the UIHearts.cs file script:

```
using Chapter6Game.Content.Objects;
using Microsoft.Xna.Framework;
using Microsoft.Xna.Framework.Content;
using Microsoft.Xna.Framework.Graphics;

namespace MiniMan.Content.Objects
{
    public  class UIHearts
     {
        public Player player = new Player();
        public Texture2D fullHeart;
        public Texture2D emptyHeart;

        public Vector2[] Positions = new Vector2[3];
        public void LoadContent(ContentManager Content)
        {
           emptyHeart = Content.Load<Texture2D>("UI/EmptyHeart");
            fullHeart = Content.Load<Texture2D>("UI/Heart");
        }

        public void Initialize()
        {
```

```
        Positions[0] = new Vector2(-795, 90);
        Positions[1] = new Vector2(-820, 90);
        Positions[2] = new Vector2(-845, 90);
    }
    public void Draw(SpriteBatch batch)
    {
        if (player.health == 3)
        {
            batch.Draw(fullHeart, Positions[0], Color.White);
            batch.Draw(fullHeart, Positions[1], Color.White);
            batch.Draw(fullHeart, Positions[2], Color.White);
        }
        else if (player.health == 2)
        {
            batch.Draw(fullHeart, Positions[0], Color.White);
            batch.Draw(fullHeart, Positions[1], Color.White);
            batch.Draw(emptyHeart, Positions[2], Color.White);
        }

        else if (player.health == 1)
        {
            batch.Draw(fullHeart, Positions[0], Color.White);
            batch.Draw(emptyHeart, Positions[1], Color.White);
            batch.Draw(emptyHeart,Positions[2], Color.White);
        }

        else if (player.health == 0)
        {
         batch.Draw(emptyHeart, Positions[0], Color.White);
         batch.Draw(emptyHeart, Positions[1], Color.White);
         batch.Draw(emptyHeart, Positions[2], Color.White);
        }
```

```
        }
    }
}
```

Now you have to update the Draw() and Initialize() methods of the hearts in your GameRoot.cs. Don't forget to set the UIHearts class as an object above:

```
Public class GameRoot : Game
{
UIHearts hearts = new UIHearts();
...
protected override void Initialize()
{
hearts.Initialize();
}
protected override void Draw(GameTime gameTime)
{
hearts.draw(_spritebatch);
}
}
```

Next, you update the InputManager's Keys.D and Keys.A statements to move the hearts around:

```
if (Input.IsPressed(Keys.A) && !player.isCollidingside)
        {
                flip = true;
                AnimState = 1;
                player.position.X -= player.speed;
                CameraPos.X -= player.speed;
                hearts.Positions[0].X -= player.speed;
                hearts.Positions[1].X -= player.speed;
```

```
                hearts.Positions[2].X -= player.speed;
        }
if (Input.IsPressed(Keys.D) && !player.isCollidingside)
            {
        flip = false;
        CameraPos.X += player.speed;
        player.position.X = player.position.X + player.speed;
        hearts.Positions[0].X += player.speed ;
        hearts.Positions[1].X += player.speed;
        hearts.Positions[2].X += player.speed ;
        AnimState = 1;
            }
```

If you run the game, you'll have hearts moving with your player. Now let's set up some simple debugging.

Setting Up For Debugging

Debugging is a useful tool for adjusting small little details and functionalities in your game, such as gravity, collision detection, and much more. In this debug method, you're going to use the numpad keys to adjust small little tidbits for your player character to help the game feel better.

It's always helpful to have a small debugging method happen in your script to test things out instead of having to go back and forth between the code base to adjust small details. You'll use the Debug.WriteLine() that comes built into the System.Diagnostics of C# to output your adjustments to see which is the best fit. You can apply this to everything in a game, from enemies to the way a camera pans and zooms, and even to resetting the game.

In the GameRoot class, go ahead and make a method and call it DebugPlayer() and add the following code:

```
public void DebugPlayer(){
if (Input.IsHeld(Keys.NumPad0))
            {
            player.speed -= 1 ;
            Debug.WriteLine("Speed: " + player.speed);
            }
            if (Input.IsHeld(Keys.NumPad1))
            {
            player.speed += 1;
            Debug.WriteLine("Speed: " + player.speed);
            }
            if (Input.IsPressed(Keys.NumPad2))
            {
            player.gravity--;
            Debug.WriteLine("Gravity: " + player.gravity);
            }
            if (Input.IsPressed(Keys.NumPad3))
            {
                player.gravity++;
                Debug.WriteLine( "Gravity:  " + player.gravity);
            }

            if (Input.IsHeld(Keys.NumPad4))
            {
        player.playerRect.Width--;
        Debug.WriteLine( "Width: " + player.playerRect.Width);
            }
            if (Input.IsHeld(Keys.NumPad5))
            {
```

```
            player.playerRect.Width++;
            Debug.WriteLine("Width: " +  player.playerRect.
            Width);
    }
    if (Input.IsHeld(Keys.NumPad6))
    {
player.playerRect.Height--;
Debug.WriteLine("Height: " + player.playerRect.
Height);
    }
    if (Input.IsHeld(Keys.NumPad7))
    {
player.playerRect.Height++;
Debug.WriteLine("Height: " + player.playerRect.
Height);
    }
}
```

If you run this code, you can see the values of each of the variables being changed in the Console Output Window in Visual Studio. It's better to keep this method separate from the actual Update() method in order to save on CPU memory and to only call it when necessary. You can also use this same sort of method to bind to other keys and test for other objects like Enemies and other objects within the scene.

Conclusion

In this chapter, you learned why scripting is used, how you can use it to make objects interact with each other, and what you can do to make the development process easier. In the next chapter, you will go over enemy AI and how to make a boss battle. You'll then spend the remaining chapters polishing your little game by adding menus, sounds, and particle effects.

For this chapter, you can find the current game on GitHub through this link:

```
https://github.com/RamiMorrar/MiniManPart1
```

CHAPTER 6

Enemy AI and Algorithms

So you can now move around in your scene with the player. The character can collect coins, punch, run, and jump. They cannot, however, be hit and don't have any real obstacles to go through. This is where your enemies come in. You will have two enemy types and a boss at the end of the level.

In order to understand basic enemy logic, you must understand how to implement it first. For your player, you use an input manager to store and hold your key inputs to make him move. For your enemies, you must use conditional and algorithmic logic to make them function properly. Say, for instance, you want your enemy to stand idly and then start moving when it sees the player. You can't use the `KeyboardState` struct to make that happen because that wouldn't make any sense and is not true AI.

What you need to do to make even simple behavior such as a patrolling enemy is to understand and use formula logic to work into your conditional statements to get the enemy to move. You'll be going over several key movement patterns and you will be implementing one of them to fit in the logic of your game.

Figure 6-1 shows a breakdown of what your goals are for accomplishing good enemy AI.

© Louis Salin and Rami Morrar 2022
L. Salin and R. Morrar, *Game Development with MonoGame*,
https://doi.org/10.1007/978-1-4842-7771-3_6

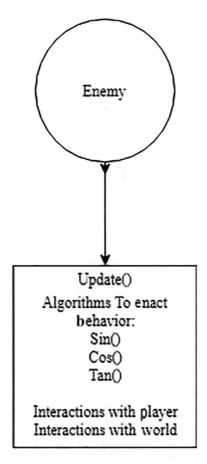

Figure 6-1. *A diagram showing what is needed for an enemy class'*
behavior

Essential Mathematics for Game Movement Logic

If you have played any 2D game, chances are you've probably encounter
several variants of enemy logic patterns. Some enemies move in a simple
straight line, others move in a wavy up-and-down motion, and others move
in more complex patterns such as circle or diamond/square motions.

Let's break down some of the more complex ones first to see how they work in certain formulas.

Sine

In mathematics, the sine is a trigonometric function of an angle and is the product of a triangle's opposite to its hypotenuse. Sine is used for various game development movement patterns and a* pathfinding. So how does sine apply to enemy scripting? You aren't calculating any triangles in your code.

True. You aren't doing any triangle drawing or anything like that in your code. But sine is a big help in basic 2D games like yours in order to provide various movement patterns. You must first inspect the basic sine formula.

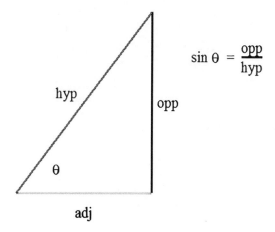

$$\sin \theta = \frac{\text{opp}}{\text{hyp}}$$

As you can see in this triangle, sine is a product of the opposite side and hypotenuse of a square. And in its basic state, there really isn't much in the way of real-life applications for sine. This is far from the case when it comes to physics. Say you want to calculate the exact amount of force and gravity needed to make an enemy float around in a wavy and linear pattern. You can use sine to adjust the rate and threshold of said wave, also known as a sine wave.

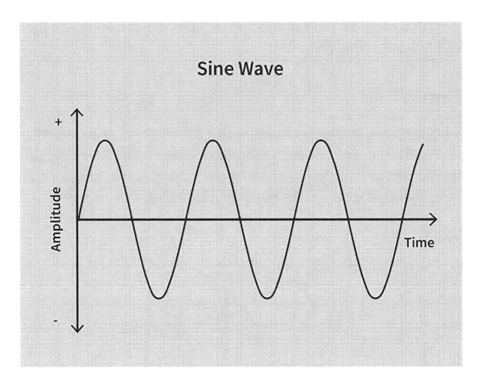

And here is its corresponding formula:

$$y = A \sin\left(2\pi f\, t + \theta\right)$$

Let's break this formula down a bit:

- A = Amplitude of the wave
- F = Frequency of the wave
- Ø = The degrees of the triangle
- t = The time of the wave's length

Using this formula in programming, you can use a speed variable and an enemy's Vector2.Y to apply it as a movement pattern.

Thankfully in your case, you don't have to write out this equation since C# already has a built-in sine formula using this namespace:

```
using System;
```

So all you really need to do now is call that formula and use it in a way that makes your enemies move as such. Let's say in your flying enemy's Update() method you want it to move in a rapid and short wave going left. In this instance, you will write something like:

```
Enemy.pos.X -= Enemy.speed;
Enemy.pos.Y = (float)MathF.Sin( (float)gameTime.TotalGameTime.
TotalMilliseconds/100);
```

Looking at this code, you already have a speed variable set with your Enemy.speed variable set to move forward. You are passing in an amount of GameTime for amplitude and dividing it by 100 for greater frequency. You don't need to include a declaration of ø anywhere because MathF.Sin() is calculating that for you. Do keep in mind that you may have to convert a few variables here and there to avoid compiler errors.

This method is very useful for enemy variety and is much less computational intensive than using your own formula. You can also set the opposite to be true for enemy.pos.X and pass in an enemy.speed for a vertical sine wave.

"But what about other physical motions? How do you get that physical behavior to be a circle?" Glad you have that thought in your head, as you'll be taking a look at those patterns now, starting with circles.

Circular Motions Using Sine and Cosine

If sine had an opposite doppelganger, it'd be cosine. Cosine is used to calculate the product of an adjacent angle as a hypotenuse. In short, it's sine but inverted. You can even change the above code from `MathF.Sin()` to `MathF.Cos()` and get a similar result. But why is this important to know? Because by combining two triangles, you can make a circle. Allow us to explain.

Here you have a unit circle:

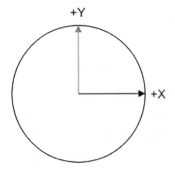

It's a pretty standard shape with equal x- and y- axes. But now let's draw a line between the green and red arrows.

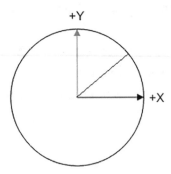

You have made a triangle. And what can you get from this triangle? That's right: a hypotenuse, opposite side, and adjacent side! Now if you take the sine and cosine of this triangle, they would be identical but inverted wavelengths So if you take the sine of cosine and cosine of sine, you get a similar result.

So what does that mean? If you make your two Vector2 floats (X,Y) use a sine and cosine function for your two floats, respectively, you can invert their amplitude and get a circle rotation!

This is what the implementation of the sine function of X and the cosine function of Y would look like in C#/MonoGame:

```
public class Enemy {
Float speed = 2;
Vector2 position;

Public Enemy() {
Position = new Vector2(0,100)
}

Public void Update(GameTime gameTime){
Position.X -= (float)MathF.Cos((float)gameTime.TotalGameTime.
TotalMilliseconds / 900) * speed;
Position.Y += (float)MathF.Sin( (float)gameTime.TotalGameTime.
TotalMilliseconds / 900)  * speed;
}
}
```

Now that you have circular and sinusoid motion, let's discuss some simple patrolling logic which you will use for your game. It's actually very simple and you can use it for all your simple enemies in your game.

Using The Distance Formula To Enable Behavior

This formula requires a bit of simple math and is very easy to adjust within the realm of a 2D space. You will use a well-known formula known as the Pythagorean Theorem:

$$c^2 = a^2 + b^2$$

This formula is very helpful for 2D side scrollers like your game because it allows you to calculate the distance between two points to give you smooth and predictable behavior with your simpler patrol enemies. But you must adjust your formula to properly take into account the distance between your player and the enemies' positions. It'll look a little something like this:

$$d = \sqrt{\left(x_2 - x_1\right)^2 + \left(y_2 - y_1\right)^2}$$

The d in the formula stands for distance. And with that distance, you can use a condition statement to see if the player is moving towards the player within the enemy's `Update()` method to return your calculation. You can use two given points, such as your `Vector2`s from your player and enemies, to make it so that this interaction actually happens. So your formula will end up looking something like this:

$$\sqrt{\left(player.pos.y - enemy.pos.y\right)^2 + \left(player.pos.x - enemy.pos.x\right)^2}$$

As you can see, you are calculating your player's and enemies' positions in your world to calculate the distance between them. You could simplify this further in your game and make it so that you only need the x coordinate from your game objects and get the same result. This way, if the player jumps too high, the enemies will not stop. This also helps optimize your code. The end result will look something like this:

$$\sqrt{\left(player.position.x - enemy.position.x\right)^2}$$

Using this formula, you can make your enemy types simply patrol when the distance is less than a given number. Fortunately, you don't have to write this formula into C# code on your own. MonoGame has a MathHelper class with a Distance() method that takes two other floats:

```
public static float Distance(float value1, float value2)
        {
            return Math.Abs(value1 - value2);
        }
```

You can use this function to express the relationship between your player and your red/blue enemies like so:

```
float distance = MathHelper.Distance(player.position.X,
Position.X);
            if (distance <= 100)
            {
                ispatroling = true;
                Position.X -= speed;
            }
```

You will also do this with your blue enemy. You will also be updating GameRoot to make it so that your enemy moves with an animation during this with a Boolean:

```
if (redEnemy.ispatroling == true)
        {
        redEnemy.anim = redAnimations[1];
        }
```

There is one more type of motion you could do. You could use this to make your own unique motion in any other shape, like a square or rectangle. This requires a bit of different logic as it has more to do with origin points, but still uses the `Distance()` method mentioned above.

Other Non-Linear Motion

So say you want to make an enemy move other than in a straight line or a circle. That is pretty simple. With the `Distance()` method, you can set an origin `Vector2` of your enemy (the location where the enemy is located) and take the x and y values of each origin and your enemy's current location to manipulate them into moving how you want. Say you want an enemy to travel forward from the right, go up from a certain position, and then travel forward again while in the air. You can do this with the `Distance()` formula. Figure 6-2 visualizes our explanation.

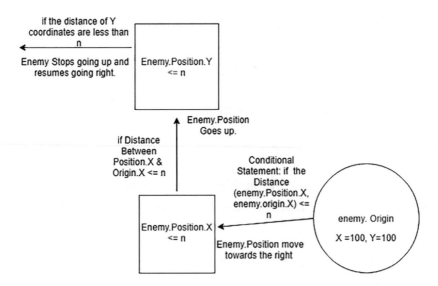

Figure 6-2. Non-linear motion

This looks complicated but it is actually very simple when you look at the code. All you need are two local float variables in the enemy's `Update()` method that calculate the distance between the coordinates of the enemy's position and origin:

```
float distancebtwnX = MathHelper.Distance(Position.X,
origin.X);
float distancebtwnY = MathHelper.Distance(Position.Y, origin.Y) ;
```

You then take these variables and add them to your conditional statements to get the movement patterns you want in your game. This code makes the enemy go from left to up to left again like a staircase:

```
//Non-Linear Movement Script That makes a staircase motion
if (distancebtwnX <= 100)
{
Position.X -= speed;
}
else if (distancebtwnY <= 200)
{
Position.Y -= speed + 2;
Debug.WriteLine("Go Up");
}
else if (distancebtwnY >= 199)
{
Position.X -= speed + 2;
Debug.WriteLine("Go Left Again");
}
```

If you play this code, the enemy will start from its origin position and update where it is going based on the distance between its origin and position.

That is all the basic enemy AI behavior we will cover here. The non-linear method is a bit difficult to wrap your head around at first, but when you understand how distance logic works, you should be able to get some good patterns going. We've commented out the functions above and commented what they are for your convenience. They will all be located in the RedEnemy's Update() method and right here:

```
// Red Enemy's Update Method:

public void Update(GameTime gameTime)
        {
                // Every function talked about in the book

                // Sinusoid Motion
                //Enemy.pos.X -= Enemy.speed;
                // Enemy.pos.Y = (float)MathF.Sin((float)gameTime.
                    TotalGameTime.TotalMilliseconds / 100);

                // Circular Motion
                //Position.X -= (float)MathF.Cos((float)gameTime.
                    TotalGameTime.TotalMilliseconds / 900) * speed;
                //Position.Y += (float)MathF.Sin((float)gameTime.
                    TotalGameTime.TotalMilliseconds / 900) * speed;

                ////Non-Linear Movement Script That makes a
                    staircase motion
                ///
                //float distancebtwnX = MathHelper.
                    Distance(Position.X, origin.X);
                //float distancebtwnY = MathHelper.
                    Distance(Position.Y, origin.Y) ;
                //Debug.WriteLine(distancebtwnX);
                //  Debug.WriteLine(distancebtwnY);
```

```
//if (distancebtwnX <= 100)
//    Position.X -= speed;
// Debug.WriteLine("Go Left");
//else if (distancebtwnY <= 200)
//{
//    Position.Y -= speed + 2;
//    Debug.WriteLine("Go Up");
//} else if (distancebtwnY >= 199)
//{

//    Position.X -= speed + 2;
//    Debug.WriteLine("Go Left Again");

//}
```

```
// Calculates the distance between player and Enemy
  float distance = MathHelper.Distance(player.position.X,
  Position.X) / (float)gameTime.TotalGameTime.TotalSeconds + 10;
 // Debug.WriteLine(distance);
```

```
        //Regular Movement
        if (distance <= 100)
        {
            ispatroling = true;
            Position.X -= speed;
            Debug.WriteLine(Position);
        }

        mainBody.X = (int)Position.X;
        mainBody.Y = (int)Position.Y;
        topofHead.X = (int)Position.X;
        topofHead.Y = (int)Position.Y;
```

```
if(mainBody.Intersects(player.playerRect))
{
    player.health--;
    Debug.WriteLine("Collision");
}
if (mainBody.Intersects(terrain.collisionRect[0]))
{
    gravity = 0;
}
else
{
    gravity = 2;
}

if (topofHead.Intersects(player.playerRect ) &&
player.hasjumped)
{
    gravity = 0;
}
anim.Position = Position;
anim.Update(gameTime);
Position.Y += gravity;
    }
}
```

Now let's talk about making an attack function for your player's punch attack to be able to defeat the blue enemy in the level.

Interactions with the Player

In order for your enemies to interact with your player, you must use your GameRoot's Update() method to do so. This is because every enemy in your field is only accessible through that new instance of the GameRoot's version of the enemy. There is a workaround to this by referencing the instance of GameRoot in the enemy's constructor like so (using the samurai boss as an example):

```
public SamuraiBoss(GameRoot root)
      {
      Position = new Vector2(875, 254);
      }
```

Now you just need to set the instances of those your enemies to your GameRoot constructor:

```
public GameRoot()
      {
            Input = new InputManager(this);
            _graphics = new GraphicsDeviceManager(this);
            Content.RootDirectory = "Content";
            IsMouseVisible = true;
            coin = new Coins(this);
            redEnemy = new RedEnemy(this);
            blueEnemy = new BlueEnemy(this);
            samurai = new SamuraiBoss(this);
      }
```

In your HandleAnimations() method of GameRoot, the following code lets you interact with the enemies:

```
if (player.playerRect.Intersects(redEnemy.mainBody))
{
```

```
getHit.Play();
//  player.health--;
//player.anim = animations[4];
}

if (player.playerRect.Intersects(blueEnemy.topofHead))
{
//player.health--;
player.position.X -= player.speed * 1.5f;
getHit.Play()
}

if(player.playerRect.Intersects(redEnemy.topofHead) && player.
hasjumped)
{
EnemyHitSound.Play();
redEnemy.mainBody.Height = 0;
redEnemy.mainBody.Width = 0;
redEnemy.topofHead.Width = 0;
redEnemy.topofHead.Height = 0;
player.position.Y -= player.speed * 6;
redEnemy.anim = redAnimations[2];
redEnemy.speed = 0;
}

if (player.fistRect.Intersects(blueEnemy.mainBody) && Input.
IsPressed(Keys.K))
{
EnemyHitSound.Play();
blueEnemy.ishit = true;
player.fistRect.Width = 0
player.fistRect.Height = 0;
}
```

As you can see, your enemies are interacting with your player through their own independent rectangles. Each conditional statement is making it so that the rectangles are causing each object to affect its own base rectangle. If you run the game, you should see that when you stomp on the red enemy and punch the blue enemy, they disappear. And that's all she wrote when it comes to the interactions. As you can see, enemy behavior can be as simple or as complex as you want it to be. If you are up for it, we recommend trying the following challenges:

- Make an enemy interact with another enemy in some way.

- Use sine, cosine, and tangent to make unique pattern motions.

- Create different variations of the same enemy.

Let's move onto the boss. What is so different about a boss? For simplicity's sake, let's make your boss just move and jump around and hit: a more advanced patrol, so to speak, with a few extra steps, like "contextual" patterns and controlled randomization.

Bosses and Patterns

To give a brutally simple explanation to what a boss is design-wise, a boss in a game is a more difficult enemy that tries to beat the player with either "random" or varied attack patterns. These "random" attack patterns of a boss aren't actually random. In fact, it's kind of like a spinning ball lottery but the machine only has five balls being spun around and you know the actual numbers of the balls. The only thing that is random is which ball will come out. It's the same thing with a typical enemy boss: a chosen attack out a handful of other attacks that are chosen at random. See Figure 6-3 for a helpful diagram to visualize it.

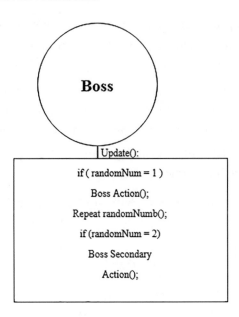

Figure 6-3. *The actions of a boss*

A boss can also be "context sensitive," meaning that there can be certain conditional statements that make the boss trigger a certain behavior. If the player is right next to a boss in their attack range, with the Distance() method, you could make it so that the boss hits the player with a really powerful attack for standing too close. The same could be said if the player is too far away. This requires a more elaborate design but is pretty straightforward, as demonstrated by Figure 6-4.

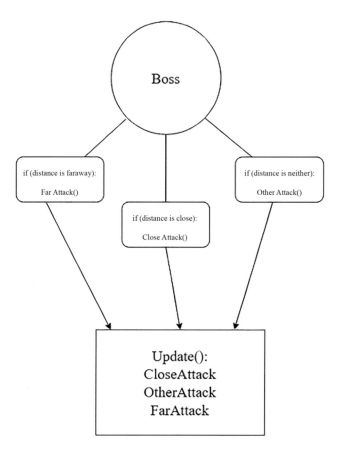

Figure 6-4. *Context-sensitive boss moves*

Usually bosses like these have a variety of different ranged attacks to keep the player on their toes. Since your boss is on a bit of terrain that could fall off and has limited space to move, let's use the second method to ensure that they'll stay inbounds and attack whenever the player is close. The full class is here:

```
public class SamuraiBoss
    {
        public bool isdead = false;
        public int health = 3;
```

```csharp
    public SpriteAnimation anim;
    public Vector2 Position;
    public Rectangle mainBody, SamuraiSlash;
   public bool walking = false;
    public bool flip = false;
    public bool isattacking = false;

    public SamuraiBoss(GameRoot root)
    {
        Position = new Vector2(700, 230);
    }
    public void Initialize()
    {
        mainBody = new Rectangle((int)Position.X, (int)
        Position.Y, 100, 48);
        SamuraiSlash = new Rectangle((int)Position.X - 10,
        (int)Position.Y, 0, 0);
    }
    public void Update(GameTime gameTime)
    {

        if (health != 0)
        {
        WalkLeftAndRight(gameTime);
        Attack(gameTime);
        }
       if (health <= 0)
        {
            isattacking = false;
            walking = false;
            isdead = true;
            Position.Y += 2;
```

```
        }
        anim.Position = Position;
        anim.Update(gameTime);
    }
    public void WalkLeftAndRight(GameTime gametime)
    {
        float x = MathF.Cos(0.8f * (float)gametime.
        TotalGameTime.TotalSeconds) * 2;

    Debug.WriteLine(Position);
    Position.X -= x;
    walking = true;
    // Add Sprite Flipping Logic Here
    if (Position.X <= 685 )
    {
     flip = true;
    }
    else {
     flip = false;
     }
  }

public void Attack(GameTime gameTime)
  {
    float distance = Vector2.Distance(Player.position,
    Position);
    Debug.WriteLine(distance);
    if (distance <= 1400)
    {
    walking = false;
    isattacking = true;
    SamuraiSlash.Width = 30;
```

```
    SamuraiSlash.Height = 30;
  }
 }
 }
```

As you can see, you put all your conditional logic for when the boss is attacking into separate methods. You then set the Boolean values in these methods to change the animations and input collision logic in your GameRoot's HandleAnimationCollisions() method:

```
if (player.fistRect.Intersects(samurai.mainBody))
            {
                Debug.WriteLine("Boss Hit");
                player.fistRect = Rectangle.Empty;
                EnemyHitSound.Play();
                samurai.health -= 1;
            }

if (player.playerRect.Intersects(samurai.SamuraiSlash))
            {
                Debug.WriteLine("Slashed");
                //player.health -= 1;
                 player.position.X -= 3;
                 hasHitPlayer = true;
            }
            if (samurai.isdead)
            {
              samurai.anim = samuraiAnimations[3];
            }
            if (samurai.isattacking)
            {
             samurai.anim = samuraiAnimations[2];
            }
```

If you run the game now and press play, you should see the boss act how you have it set it to act. It's running around and attacking as it should.

Conclusion

Congratulations, you finished programming your enemies and your boss! You still have a lot more to work on but the core gameplay is done. In this chapter you learned

- How to instantiate enemy AI

- How different mathematical functions can allow the behavior you want

- How using different methods can help make for a compelling boss

In the next chapter, you'll cover game menus and gamepad support.

CHAPTER 7

Game State and Gamepad Input

You have done what is necessary for the base of your game so now you need to build around it. You can't just have the player start off in the middle of the game, and you want your player to play with more than just a keyboard. Let's make a main menu and code in a gamepad controller. You'll start with the gamepad input detection.

Gamepad Detection

MonoGame natively supports Xbox 360 controllers in the framework, so you'll be using one to map out the input for your game. Since your game is primarily only two buttons and three directions, you really only need to program the analog stick, D-pad, and four face buttons (A, B, X, and Y). Let's write some code to get this going. Add this line of code right under the InputManager class reference in the GameRoot.cs file where your global variables are located:

```
GamePadCapabilities capabilities = GamePad.
GetCapabilities(PlayerIndex.One);
```

© Louis Salin and Rami Morrar 2022
L. Salin and R. Morrar, *Game Development with MonoGame*,
https://doi.org/10.1007/978-1-4842-7771-3_7

And in the update method, put the following code logic into your game. You update each of the buttons along with the D-pad and Left Analog to have your player character move left or right, as well as jump and punch:

```
#region Controller Input
if (capabilities.IsConnected)
{
    AnimStates();

    GamePadState state = GamePad.GetState
    (PlayerIndex.One);
    if (state.IsButtonDown(Buttons.B))
    {
        AnimState = 3;
    }
    if (state.IsButtonDown(Buttons.Y))
    {
        AnimState = 3;
    }
    if (state.IsButtonDown(Buttons.A) && !player.
    hasjumped)
    {

        player.position.Y -= 14;
        player.gravity = -7.5f;
        player.hasjumped = true;

    }
    if (state.IsButtonDown(Buttons.X) && !player.
    hasjumped)
    {

        player.position.Y -= 14;
```

```
    player.gravity = -7.5f;
    player.hasjumped = true;

}

if (state.IsButtonDown(Buttons.DPadLeft) &&
!player.isCollidingside)
{
    flip = true;
    AnimState = 1;
    player.position.X -= player.speed;
    CameraPos.X -= player.speed;
    hearts.Positions[0].X -= player.speed;
    hearts.Positions[1].X -= player.speed;
    hearts.Positions[2].X -= player.speed;

}

if (state.IsButtonDown(Buttons.DPadRight) &&
!player.isCollidingside)
{
    flip = false;
    AnimState = 1;
    player.position.X += player.speed;
    CameraPos.X += player.speed;
    hearts.Positions[0].X += player.speed;
    hearts.Positions[1].X += player.speed;
    hearts.Positions[2].X += player.speed;
}

if (capabilities.HasLeftXThumbStick)
    {
    //Moves player with the Thumbstick
```

```
if (state.ThumbSticks.Left.X < -0.5f && !player.isCollidingside)
            {
                    flip = true;
                    AnimState = 1;
                    player.position.X -= player.speed;
                    CameraPos.X -= player.speed;
                    hearts.Positions[0].X -= player.speed;
                    hearts.Positions[1].X -= player.speed;
                    hearts.Positions[2].X -= player.speed;
            }
if (state.ThumbSticks.Left.X > .5f && !player.isCollidingside)
            {
                    flip = false;
                    AnimState = 1;
                    player.position.X += player.speed;
                    CameraPos.X += player.speed;
                    hearts.Positions[0].X += player.speed;
                    hearts.Positions[1].X += player.speed;
                    hearts.Positions[2].X += player.speed;
            }
        }
    }

    #endregion
```

If you run the game with this code in it, you will notice that your player is now able to move with an Xbox controller plugged in!

What MonoGame is doing is detecting your Xbox 360 controller's driver (a computer program that operates or controls a particular type of device that is attached to a computer) and is initiating your program to take the controller's input.

We tested other devices and interestingly even controllers for the PlayStation 4 also work. Do note that not all controllers are created equal and you might have to do some tuning to make your controller's input detection work correctly with each controller's .dll files.

Let's move on to changing screens.

Game States

Currently in your code, you only have the default game state rendering out your main level. Since your game is simple, you only really need a couple game states to render: a main menu, a screen when your player dies, and a screen for when your player wins.

The main menu is very simple. You wrap your entire GameRoot class in a Boolean. You set that Boolean to false, and when you start the game by pressing Enter, the game will be drawn out like so:

```
public class GameRoot : Game
{
bool gameStarted = false;

protected override void Update(GameTime gameTime)
{
if (Keyboard.GetState().IsKeyDown(Keys.Enter))
gameStarted = true;
}
}
```

The gameStarted bool is seen throughout the GameRoot class. When this bool is set to false, you have just your background with some text telling the player to press Enter to play the game.

```
protected override void Update (GameTime gameTime){
if (!gameStarted)
```

```
{
string title = "Mini Man";
string startText = "Press Enter To Start";
_spriteBatch.Draw(background, new Vector2(0, 0), Color.White);
_spriteBatch.DrawString(font, title, new Vector2(150, 200),
Color.Black);
_spriteBatch.DrawString(font, startText, new Vector2(115, 220),
Color.Black);
}
}
```

Next, you update the player and keys for when your player dies using the player isDead Boolean.

```
if(!playerisDead)
{
player.Update(gameTime);
}
```

You can use a different bool, playerWon, to stop the player from moving and bring up some text for when the player beats the samurai boss in your GameRoot's Draw() method. You also need to update the GameRoot's Update() method in order to stop the player from moving when playerWon is set to true:

```
Update(GameTime  gameTime)
{
...
if (!playerisDead || !playerWon)
{
player.Update(gameTime);
}
}
```

```
Draw(GameTime gameTime)
{
...
if (playerWon)
{
string Won = "Congrats, you won!";
_spriteBatch.DrawString(font, Won, CameraPos, Color.Black);
}
}
```

Conclusion

This chapter was brief but important on how to do simple game states. In the next chapter, you'll figure out how to add particles and sound effects to your game to give it some polish and finally ship out your game!

CHAPTER 8

Packaging The Game with Bells and Whistles

You are almost done completing your small platformer game. You have done a lot, from covering enemy AI behavior to making your own menu screen system. What you need to do now is give it a bit more polish by adding a bit of flare to it. Let's add some audio and a particle effects engine for your game.

Loading in Music and Sound Effects

MonoGame makes it very easy to add your own sound files. MonoGame supports three types of audio files; .wav, .mp3 and .ogg. There are some things to note about how to use them when it comes to MonoGame's audio classes. There are two primary classes used for audio: SoundEffect and Song. SoundEffect loads in .ogg and .wav files, and Song takes in .mp3 files. SoundEffect is used for instances of a situation, such as when a player jumps or an enemy gets hit. Song is used for background music and ambient sounds, like a jungle or night setting. You can load instances of your audio files in your GameRoot's LoadContent() method like so:

L. Salin and R. Morrar, *Game Development with MonoGame*,
https://doi.org/10.1007/978-1-4842-7771-3_8

```
#region Audio Load
jumpSnd = Content.Load<SoundEffect>("Fx/Jump");
CoinSnd = Content.Load<SoundEffect>("Fx/Coin");
getHit = Content.Load<SoundEffect>("Fx/GetHit");
EnemyHitSound = Content.Load<SoundEffect>("Fx/EnemyHitSound");
AttackSound = Content.Load<SoundEffect>("Fx/AttackSound");
SamuraiSlash = Content.Load<SoundEffect>("Fx/Slash");
main = Content.Load<Song>("Music/Theme");
            end = Content.Load<Song>("Music/GameOver");
            #endregion
```

Playing a song is also pretty simple. In your `Initialize()` method in GameRoot.cs, you use the `MediaPlayer` class provided by MonoGame's Media Library to play music like so:

```
MediaPlayer.Play(main);
```

Sound effects have their own method for playing. For example, in this function for punching in the `Update()` method in GameRoot, the attack sound is played every 2/3s of a second:

```
if (Input.IsPressed(Keys.K) && punchDelay >= 0.65f)
    {
    punchDelay = 0;
    AttackSound.Play();
    }
if (Input.IsPressed(Keys.K))
 {
 AnimState = 3;
 }
```

That is all there is to it in terms of audio. Using conditional statements also makes it so that a sound effect doesn't play over and over again, as seen in the above code. You also need to adjust the collision a bit so you don't get repeating calls of the same sound effect:

```
if(player.playerRect.Intersects(redEnemy.topofHead) &&
player.hasjumped)
            {
// Makes all enemy rect properties 0 to prevent continuous
sound calls
                EnemyHitSound.Play();
                redEnemy.mainBody.Height = 0;
                redEnemy.mainBody.Width = 0;
                redEnemy.topofHead.Width = 0;
                redEnemy.topofHead.Height = 0;
                redEnemy.anim = redAnimations[2];
                redEnemy.speed = 0;                }
```

Making a Particle Emitter

For your last bit of polish, you're going to make a particle engine. The way you'll do this is by taking in some simple shape textures, such as stars and diamonds, and giving them their own physics logic to create a fast but beautiful trail for your player whenever they move or jump.

First, let's make a separate file that will contain your particle engine information for organization purposes. Let's call this file ParticleEmitter.cs and input your two classes, the Particle class and the ParticleEngine class.

```
using Microsoft.Xna.Framework;
using Microsoft.Xna.Framework.Graphics;
using System;
```

```
using System.Collections.Generic;

namespace MiniMan.Content.Objects
{
    public class Particle
    {
        public Texture2D Image { get; set; }
        public Vector2 Pos { get; set; }
        public Vector2 Velocity { get; set; }
        public float Angle { get; set; }
        public float AngularVelocity { get; set; }
        public Color Color { get; set; }
        public float Size { get; set; }
        public int LifeTime { get; set; }

        public Particle(Texture2D image, Vector2 pos, Vector2
        velocity,
            float angle, float angularVelocity, Color color,
            float size, int lifeTime)
        {
           Image = image;
            Pos = pos;
            Velocity = velocity;
            Angle = angle;
            AngularVelocity = angularVelocity;
            Color = color;
            Size = size;
            LifeTime = lifeTime;
        }

        public void Update()
        {
            LifeTime--;
```

```
        Pos -= Velocity;
        Angle-= AngularVelocity;
    }

    public void Draw(SpriteBatch sprite)
    {
        Rectangle sourceRec = new Rectangle(0, 0, Image.
        Width, Image.Height);
        Vector2 origin = new Vector2(Image.Width / 2,
        Image.Height / 2);

        sprite.Draw(Image, Pos, sourceRec, Color,
            Angle, origin, Size, SpriteEffects.None, 0f);
    }

}
public class ParticleEngine
{
    private Random rand;
    public Vector2 EmitterLoc { get; set; }

    private List<Particle> particles;
    private List<Texture2D> images;

    public ParticleEngine(List<Texture2D> images, Vector2
    emitterLoc)
    {
        EmitterLoc =  emitterLoc;
        this.images = images;
        this.particles = new List<Particle>();
        rand = new Random();
    }

    public void Update()
```

```csharp
    {
        int maxParticles = 5;

        for (int i = 0; i < maxParticles; i++)
        {
            particles.Add(NewParticle());
        }

        for (int particle = 0; particle < particles.Count;
        particle++)
        {
            particles[particle].Update();
            if (particles[particle].LifeTime <= 0)
            {
                particles.RemoveAt(particle);
                particle--;
            }
        }
    }

    private Particle NewParticle()
    {
        Texture2D texture = images[rand.Next(images.Count)];
        Vector2 emitterLocation = EmitterLoc;
        Vector2 velocity = new Vector2(
                            1f * (float)(rand.
                            NextDouble() * 1 + 0.4f),
                            1f * (float)(rand.
                            NextDouble() * 1 + 0.4f));
        float angle = 2;
        float angularVelocity = 0.1f * (float)(rand.
        NextDouble() * 1 - 1);
        Color col = new Color(
```

```
                (float)rand.NextDouble(),
                (float)rand.NextDouble(),
                (float)rand.NextDouble());
        float size = (float)rand.NextDouble();
        int LifeTime = 6 + rand.Next(5);
        return new Particle(texture, emitterLocation,
        velocity, angle, angularVelocity, col, size,
        LifeTime);
    }

    public void Draw(SpriteBatch sprite)
    {
        for (int index = 0; index < particles.Count; index++)
        {
            particles[index].Draw(sprite);
        }
    }
  }
}
```

Allow us to explain the intricacies of these two classes. Your particle class is a single particle entity that contains a texture, speed variable, and color. You also have a size variable to change the size of said texture. Every particle entity is managed by your ParticleEngine class, which gives it the location and indexes how many particles are going in and out of the scene.

The ParticleEngine isn't affecting the actual speed at which the particles move. That is only in the actual particle class itself. You need to update it so that the particles are following the player in your GameRoot class, like so:

```
public class GameRoot : Game
    {
ParticleEngine particleEngine;
```

```
Protected override void LoadContent(){
List<Texture2D> textures = new List<Texture2D>(); // Loads in
your particle textures to be used for the particle engine
textures.Add(Content.Load<Texture2D>("Particles/diamond"));
textures.Add(Content.Load<Texture2D>("Particles/star"));
particleEngine = new ParticleEngine(textures, player.position);

// Used to draw and update textures and location of particle
engine
protected override void Update (GameTime gameTime){
particleEngine.EmitterLocation = new Vector2(player.position.
X+20, player.position.Y+30);// Updates the particle engine
location to the player's position.
particleEngine.Update();
}
Protected override Draw(GameTime gameTime){
particleEngine.Draw(_spriteBatch);
}
}
}
```

If you run the game now, you'll see that the emitter location is now
following your player's location as they move! Figure 8-1 shows the result.

Figure 8-1. *A particle engine that follows the player's back*

Let's talk about what the particle engine is doing so it's easier to understand.

Lists and What They Do

The lists you are using are mainly for memory optimization. This list is constantly removing and adding the diamond and star images you are loading in. Your `ParticleEngine` class is constantly adding and removing the actual instance of every particle coming out for memory optimization. It doesn't matter how many textures you add to the list because the engine will simply remove each instance of that texture's particle from memory. So how does the direction of the particles work?

Actual Physics and the Amount of Particles Swaying

In the Particle's `Update()` method, each particle's position Vector2 is actively being moved with a velocity Vector2. In your private method, `NewParticle`, when you add a value to this velocity Vector, the speed of the particle trail is affected. If you actually change some part of that code, you get different results depending on what you put in. If you input a number more negative than the -1 seen in the code, the particles will fly like they are coming out the player's body. If you input a positive number, the particles will look like they're coming out the player's back.

As for the amount coming out per frame, if you tinker with the `ParticleEngine`'s `maxParticles` int value, you get more particles coming out as a result.

Here are two challenges you might enjoy doing:

− Try making a fire-like particle effect with different textures.

− See about adding different constructors/methods to the `Particle` class for reusable results.

Now that you're all done, let's package your game in a neat little file format to be accessed from your computer.

Packaging The Game

Publishing the game is pretty simple. It's just a few clicks in Visual Studio. Go ahead and right-click the **MiniMan** project name, as shown in Figure 8-2.

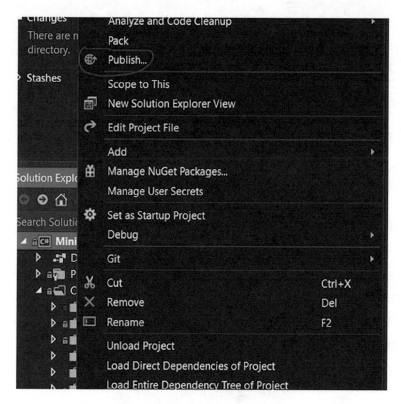

Figure 8-2. *Publishing your game*

Next, click Publish and follow the steps to publish to a local folder. You can post it anywhere but we decided to post to the folder already available. See Figure 8-3.

Figure 8-3. *Picking a Publish location*

Once you hit Publish, you should be able to see your game's .exe file with the common MonoGame icon. Congratulations, you published your first MonoGame game!

Note   If you want to change the icon of the game, all you have to do is change the `Icon.ico` file to something else. You have to keep the same name though.

Conclusion

In this book, you learned about

- Managing resource files for multiple languages

- Optimizing the game to be 60 FPS

190

– Cameras and layers

– Level editor

– Game scripting and its usefulness

– Enemy AI patterns

– Gamepad and screen management

– Enhancing the game with audio and effects

With your first game published, we bet you're excited to know what else you can do with MonoGame. In the next chapter, you'll get more great resources to show what you can do with MonoGame, along with helpful and free resources to get you started making your own games, such as audio, character sprite sheets, and UI components. We will also be talking about a few noteworthy libraries to help make your journey using MonoGame much easier, such as physics and collision detection libraries and window rendering components to help make it easier for you to make your own full-blown engine.

CHAPTER 9

Tying It All Together

Your long journey of learning the MonoGame framework has finally come to an end. You covered a lot in this book—from dev tools, such as a debug mode and a window rendering component to make a level editor, to gameplay experience enhancements, like AI and menu/UI overlays. With all this knowledge, it's now time to go out into the world and make your own game. You have this book to help you out on your journey, plus a lot of resources to help you get started on your first game. The websites and forums we list below offer a ton of free assets and ways to network with other game developers, artists, composers, and level designers.

Websites For Collaboration and Assets

Itch.io

Itch.io is a place where people can buy, sell, and host their own games without having to pay a fee for publishing. This is great for getting started because you can gather free assets made by other users and use them for your own project, get help with your game by publishing demos, network with potential artists, and overall make your development journey much easier. From playtesting help to a plethora of other development tools, Itch makes it easy to grab resources to make some great looking games.

GamedevMarket.net

Although some assets on this site have a price tag, there are a few free good assets that you can use for your game. The site is constantly being updated with new content every week, and there are some assets that definitely offer a bang for your buck.

OpenGameArt

A more underground Itch.io, OpenGameArt (OGA) has tons of resources you can use for your game under a plethora of creative licenses. OGA has its own unique set of assets as well as an astounding library of sound collections.

MonoGame.Net

The official MonoGame Forums are great places to get resources on programming knowledge from basic physics to code optimization to get that smooth 60 FPS! The forums are active daily.

In Conclusion

We hope that this book serves you well in your MonoGame journey. We wish the best of luck to you in making your own engine with this framework, and through that, making your own games. Do note that this is only the foundation of your game development journey and you can take the scope farther than we have introduced in this book. We once again strongly implore you to find more resources and research other libraries as there are a ton on GitHub that you can take from. But to end this book, we hope you enjoyed this book on behalf of the Apress staff. Have a good day and happy MonoGaming!

Index

T, U, V, W, X, Y, Z

Printed in the United States
by Baker & Taylor Publisher Services